# BALANCE

# BALANCE

## A Story of Faith, Family, and Life on the Line

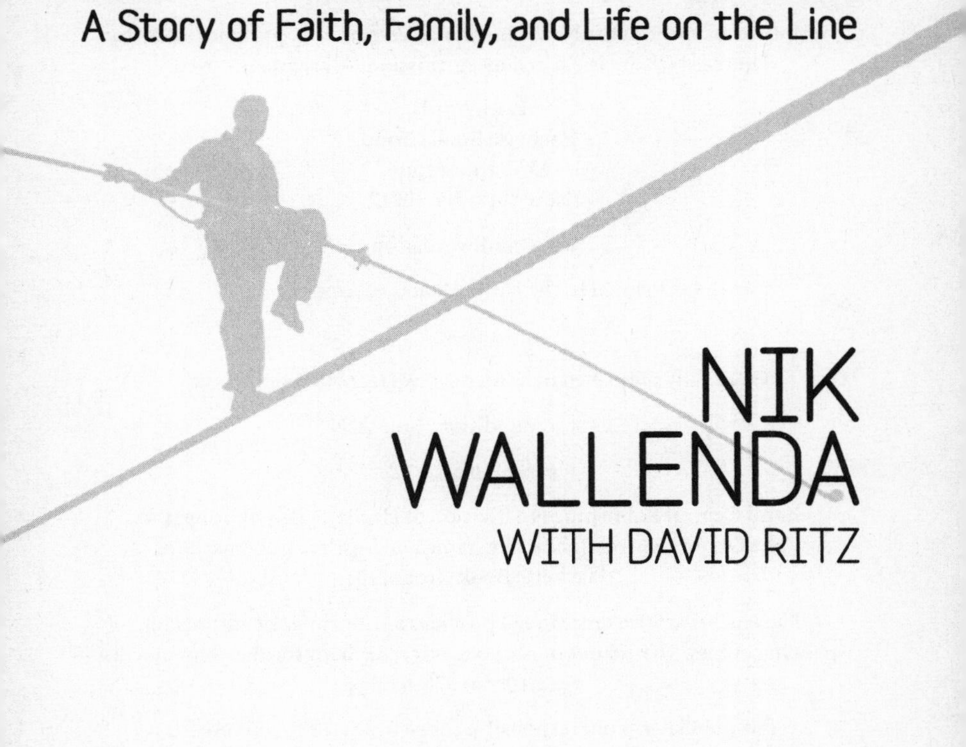

# NIK
# WALLENDA

## WITH DAVID RITZ

Faith Words

New York • Boston • Nashville

Scripture taken from the New King James Version®. Copyright © 1982 by Thomas Nelson, Inc. Used by permission. All rights reserved.

FaithWords
Hachette Book Group
237 Park Avenue
New York, NY 10017

www.faithwords.com

Printed in the United States of America

RRD-C

Originally published in hardcover by Hachette Book Group.

First trade edition: June 2014

10 9 8 7 6 5 4 3 2 1

Grand Central Publishing is a division of Hachette Book Group, Inc. The Grand Central Publishing name and logo are trademarks of Hachette Book Group, Inc.

The Hachette Speakers Bureau provides a wide range of authors for speaking events. To find out more, go to www.hachettespeakersbureau.com or call (866) 376-6591.

The publisher is not responsible for websites (or their content) that are not owned by the publisher.

Library of Congress Catalog Number: 2013934181

ISBN 978-1-4555-4549-0 (pbk.)

# CONTENTS

God is my center.

God's grace is the balancing pole that keeps me from falling into self-obsession and self-deception. Whatever I have achieved—and will ever achieve—is the result of my relationship with Him.

This book is a continuation of that relationship. I invoke His holy spirit in helping me understand my past. I need His insightful compassion to illuminate my story and the story of my remarkable family.

As God inspires me every hour of every day, I pray that the same inspiration informs every page of this book. I pray that the miracle of His limitless love touches me as I write, just as it touches you as you read.

# 1
# Dream

The first things I notice are the dogs. They're Cairn terriers, like Toto in *The Wizard of Oz,* like the terriers that Mom and Dad keep as pets, the warm and fuzzy pups that are part of my clown act. I'm a kid in this dream, a little boy on a journey whose destination is unknown. I walk through the woods. The sky is clear, the sun bright, the air clean. The dogs run ahead of me, leading the way. The woods morph into a jungle. There are chimpanzees and exotic birds perched in the trees. Wildflowers are everywhere. In the distance, I make out the trumpet cry of an elephant. I hear the growl of lions and tigers. I'm not afraid because I've been around all sorts of animals. I'm a circus kid with circus parents from whom I've inherited a circus life. Are the dogs directing me to a circus where I'll put on my clown's outfit and perform?

As the dogs charge ahead, I sprint to keep up. The jungle turns into a green meadow and the meadow leads to a mountain covered with blue and yellow wildflowers. The sounds change. The cry of the beasts transforms into the roar of raging water.

What is the source?

Where is the water?

Chasing after the pups, I run up the mountainside. The faster I run, the taller the mountain seems to grow, the louder the roar. I keep running and running, wondering if this is a trick. Is this real? Will I ever reach the top?

I finally do. I stop to catch my breath and survey the scene. Spread out before me is a natural wonder, a spectacular horseshoe-shaped waterfall commanding the width of the entire horizon.

*"Walk over the falls."*

I turn around and see the man who has spoken these words. He is dressed in the billowy white shirt and satin trousers outfit of a circus performer. His face is friendly. His voice is not stern, not frightening, but simply clear. He speaks in a tone that is matter-of-fact, repeating the words for a second time—*"Walk over the falls."*

Although the task seems impossible, the idea excites me. It seems like fun. I want to do it. I want to know how. I want to know where to set the poles and put up the cable. I want the man to instruct me. But just as I turn to him for more instruction, I wake up.

———

Over the years the dream will assume different forms, but the theme never changes. Not only am I challenged to achieve the impossible, but the challenges grow in dimension. I soon realize that the man who haunts my imagination, awake and sleeping, is Karl Wallenda, the great patriarch of the Wallenda family. He is the man who fell from the high wire to his death in Puerto Rico on March 22, 1978, ten months before my birth on January 24, 1979. He is the man who entered my dreams early in my life and has remained there ever since. He is also the man who is my mother's grandfather and my father's teacher, the man who literally brought my parents together and hired them to work in his company of performing artists.

———

Amazingly enough, one day the abstract dream becomes concrete reality when my parents are performing at the Shrine Circus in Buffalo. That's when they take their two children to Niagara Falls. I'm six and my sister Lijana is eight. We spend months at a time on the road and on days off often visit places of interest like the Washington Monument or the field where the Battle of Gettysburg was fought. I like these tourist excursions. I find them fascinating. But Niagara is something else altogether. I'm not only stunned by its tremendous size, but thrilled to be facing an awesome sight that seems to have emerged from my dream.

"I've been here before," I tell my dad.

"You must have seen pictures, son," he says. "We've never been here before."

"I have."

Dad laughs off my remarks, but I cling to the memory. As we drive from the American side to Canada for a closer look at the rushing waters cascading some twenty stories down into the Niagara River, I relive my dream. My heart beats like crazy. I don't feel at all crazy. I feel connected. I feel centered. I don't know what to call these feelings. I don't know how to describe the excitement coursing through me. I don't know words like "destiny" and "purpose." My parents have taught us that all good things come from God, so I do know that this sensation of being connected to my dreams has to be good. I know that God has to be at the center of my imagination that is constructing a wire across the Falls. In my mind, I see myself walking from one country to another. Even as a child, I realize that the vision isn't mine. It has come to me in a dream. It has come to me from a relative I have never known. But now I am standing before it, my face wet from the spray of water. My eyes are wet with tears of joy.

I know what I have to do.

I know I will do it.

But in doing it—not in a dream, not in the imagination of a child, but in real time before millions of television viewers the world over—I will require two and a half decades of learning. Those lessons engage the mind but mostly they engage the spirit. The lessons involve steely determination. Yet the source of that determination is God.

Without Him, there is no journey, no lesson, no dream.

# 2

# Two Feet

Look at the little kid in the backyard of his parents' house in Sarasota, Florida.

You won't be impressed by the surroundings. Though his mom and dad are well-known circus performers and part of the legendary Wallenda clan, they live modestly. The scruffy working-class neighborhood has an almost rural feel. Scattered around the yard is the training gear— the various poles, posts, and bars—that aerialists use to hone their skills and develop new stunts. The object that captivates the kid is a cable some twenty-four inches off the ground strung between two stands. The kid is fixated on the cable. The kid is barely two years old. The kid is me.

My earliest and strongest memory is stepping out on the wire with the absolute conviction that I would walk across it. I have already seen my parents walk the high wire, an act that seems both wonderful and natural. Naturally I'm moved to do the same.

I take a couple of steps, and then fall.

I get back on, only to fall again.

I keep getting on and keep falling, getting on and falling until in a short while I'm able to walk the entire length of the wire. The accomplishment does not feel remarkable. I don't feel that I've had done anything extraordinary. It simply feels right.

The length of the wire isn't long—just a few yards. I wish it were longer. All that morning and well into early afternoon I keep walking back and forth. I've found my footing. I'm a restless and superenergetic child, yet this short walk over a cable has calmed me down and sent me into a state of inexplicable concentration, hardly typical of someone my age. No doubt about it; I've found this magical comfort zone in which time is suspended.

"Time to come in!" Mom shouts.

But I'm not about to come in. I shout back, "I did it! Did you see how good I did it?"

"Of course you did it! You did it beautifully!"

"I wanna keep doing it."

"You need to eat, Nik."

"I need to keep doing it."

"You will. You have the rest of your life to do it."

—

But would I?

All I knew then was the joy of a boy who had found the greatest toy in the world. What I didn't know was that my parents were barely making a living. I didn't know that the traditional circus circuit was on the verge of collapse. For all the satisfaction that came with their life as entertainers, they continually faced financial ruin. Circuses were going bankrupt. Premier performers with sterling reputations, Mom and Dad were forced to take all sorts of odd jobs—washing windows, working in restaurants—to keep a roof over our heads. Whatever precocious talents I might have displayed at an early age, they had no hope for my future in a field that had sustained the Wallenda family for over two hundred years. Understandably, they saw this as the end of the line. In fact, the title of the book about my mom's life was *The Last of the Wallendas.*

In the first two decades of my life I became increasingly aware of a dark cloud hanging over circus life. From that first step on the wire at age two, it was my passion, but a passion born at a time of impending death. Even when there was a reinvention of sorts—the explosion of Cirque du Soleil in the nineties—that Canadian phenomenon had little effect on my parents and the old-school venues that were rapidly disappearing. The wolf remained at our door.

I offer none of this in the way of complaint. Being born into struggle is a blessing. That struggle gave me an extra measure of motivation—and for that I'm grateful. That struggle tested my commitment to the aerial art form I love so deeply. That struggle also made me dependent on God. It didn't take long to realize that I couldn't win the struggle without leaning on a source of strength no human could supply.

My parents helped me realize that at an early age. Practicing Christians, they were devoted to their children. Through their example, I accepted Christ as a child. But

I also found myself absorbing their very human fears and anxieties. They couldn't guide me past their own fears and anxieties. Only God could.

In the same way, only God could give me the insight and strength to turn my long family lineage, marked by deadly tragedies, to triumph. To an alarming degree, that lineage is also marked by betrayal, backbiting, and mean-spirited jealousy. Yet my lineage is a miraculous blessing—as long as I view it through the eyes of a grateful child of God.

I believe that God gives us the power to transform any story from darkness to light. He has taught me how the stories of my forebears, no matter how painful, can benefit my life and the lives of my children. He has shown me how negative can be rebirthed as positive. To tell that story, though, the negatives cannot be overlooked. To show the miracle of transformation—the movement from despair to hope—the despair must be revealed. The truth must be told.

As a young child, I loved fairy tales. I looked at the Wallenda family saga as something of a fairy tale. Karl Wallenda, the man who excited my imagination, was a hero. He remains so to this day. I continue to derive sustenance from his never-say-die example of optimism. I never tire of quoting his mantra: "Life is on the wire; everything else is just waiting."

I view my great-grandfather as a man of boundless courage and fortitude. I've never seen him as a competitor, but only an inspiration. It is never my intention to overshadow his feats. They remain remarkable. But as I have come of age, I have learned that, unlike some mythic character out of a fairy tale, Karl Wallenda was made of flesh and blood.

As a family man, he suffered through a long series of spectacular failures. His private life resulted in chaos and confusion for those close to him. That chaos filtered down to his daughter Jenny, my grandmother, and Jenny's daughter Delilah, my mother. These women were deeply hurt. They bore emotional scars. Those scars had enormous impact on me. They are part of my story.

To tell any story with honesty and candor, scars cannot be hidden. Scars must be shown. If scars are to heal, they must be attended to. There's no way, for example, to understand the story of Christ without seeing His scars. If His scars are airbrushed out, we miss the message. His scars are the means by which we comprehend His undying love for us. His scars are the means by which we *feel* His undying love for us. His scars are part of God's instructional plan, symbols of how human pain can lead to divine glory.

For me, Jesus' story is the big one. It's the story that says even the most brutal and tortuous ending isn't an ending at all but merely the beginning of forever. It's the one that says that lies can turn to truth and death can turn to life.

So I will do my best to reveal all scars and shortcomings—especially my own—without assigning blame or wallowing in self-pity. I will do my best, through my own limited understanding, to briefly tell the story that little Nik, walking a wire a few feet off the ground, could never have known. This gutsy kid—happy, hyper, fun loving—had no idea of the monumental saga that was, in fact, his legacy. Looking to stay on the wire, trying to find balance, he was blissfully unaware of how the history of the man in his dreams would shape his own life.

# 3
# The Struggle

Karl Wallenda's great-grandfather Johannes was an acrobat. So was his namesake, his grandfather Karl. His father, Englebert, was an animal trainer as well as a celebrated aerialist.

Karl Wallenda, born in Germany in 1905, had it in his blood. It was an impassioned boiling blood, even a violent blood. His older brother Herman and young brother Willy feared their father's trigger temper. At age four, Karl experienced Englebert's brutality. In punishment for a minor infraction, his dad threw him to the ground and for the rest of his life Karl remained half-deaf in his right ear.

Karl's older brother Herman said that Englebert "was kinder to animals than he was people." Yet Karl also admired his father's artistry. Englebert was the first to bring a flying trapeze act, an innovation developed in the United States, to Europe. Admiration was intermingled with fear.

When Karl was six, Englebert abandoned the family. Karl and Willy were placed in a Catholic boarding school while Herman stayed with Englebert to perform in the father's traveling circus.

After twelve months away from his parents, Karl returned to his mother Kunigunde—as did brother Herman. But Willy was whisked off by Englebert to perform as a member of his troupe. Mama Kunigunde, the daughter of a noted ballerina from Berlin's Staats Theater, was a gifted performer in her own right. Her claim to fame was an ability on the slack wire to use her teeth to pick up a handkerchief—all this as she daintily spun an umbrella overhead.

Two years after Englebert left Mama Kunigunde, she married a circus colleague sixteen years her junior, George Grotefant, with whom she would have two children. A musician, clown, contortionist, and acrobat, George displayed talent for all aspects of circus entertainment except money management. George and Mama Kunigunde combined resources to form a troupe of entertainers seeking work in rural Western Europe.

In 1913, as war clouds gathered, the family fell into abject poverty. Their circus wagon broke down in a small German village. George was conscripted into the army. Herman was working at a munitions plant. Karl was teased and beaten because the Wallenda name was Czech in origin, not German. He challenged his tormentors with a wager—that he could climb the church steeple and do a headstand on the revolving weathercock. In an act of great daring, he won the bet hands down. He did this at age nine.

At age ten, with his stepfather and brothers gone, Karl

became his mother's sole breadwinner. In the tiny town of Gros Ottersleben he worked as a street performer for spare change to stave off his family's starvation. George survived the war and the troupe—the Wallenda-Grotefant circus— was reassembled, but postwar Germany was in ruins. Rather than walk on high, Karl found himself walking below ground. He was forced to take a job in a run-down coal mine. The work nearly drove him mad. A season with a traveling circus restored his sanity. He worked as a clown and trapeze artist. Karl perfected his astounding hand-stands and chair stands. He devised a unique way to fix his arms and legs in two rings suspended in space, a visual suggestion of a crucified Christ. He worked in the same show as Marlene Dietrich, still a teenager. They met and spoke for the first and only time in their lives.

At sixteen, Karl broke from his family and traveled to Breslau to join the circus of Louis Weitzmann—a womanizing tyrant—who saw Karl's high-wire potential. The Weitzmann troupe traveled to Budapest, where Karl's confidence grew. Before long he left the despot and ventured out on his own.

He didn't leave alone. His companion was a colleague, ten years his senior, known professionally as Princess Magneta, "The Levitating Marvel." The blonde beauty in a magician's act, she was Magdalena Schmidt, called Lena by her friends. Together they fled Weitzmann's company and found work with Max "The Human Kite" Zimmerman, whose troupe traveled to Leipzig.

In 1923 Karl and Lena switched to the Strassburger Circus as the company toured Austria and ventured over the

Bavarian Alps. Karl, at age eighteen, became more audacious on the high wire. He insisted on performing without
a net. He taught Lena tricks on the sway pole. He reunited
with brother Herman and stepfather George to form the
Wallenda Circus that traveled to Italy, where they rivaled
the Cristanis, another famous family act. In short order,
though, the Wallenda Circus went bust, even as Karl's high-
wire exploits expanded in daring and design—along with
his amorous desires.

In Berlin, working for Circus Busch, Karl fell in love with
Martha Schepp, a fifteen-year-old ballerina. When Lena
learned of the betrayal, she tried to slash Karl's throat and
disfigure Martha's face with sulfuric acid. Lena finally left,
but Martha, who feared the high wire, could not replace her
in the act. Besides, Martha was pregnant. That same year
Karl married her.

But also in that same year Helen Kreis replaced Martha,
both on the high wire and in bed. Helen was young, beautiful, and talented. She, Karl, and Herman traveled to Cuba
where the Wallendas were booked for three months. Meanwhile, back in Germany, in 1927 a daughter was born to Karl
and Martha—Jenny Wallenda, my maternal grandmother.

In 1928, John Ringling, famed owner of the Ringling
Brothers Circus, invited Karl Wallenda and his troupe to
perform in America. Hoping to win his love back, Martha
took infant Jenny to the United States to rejoin the troupe.
Karl allowed this. According to my grandmother, her dad
embraced her and said, "Jenny, one day we will perform
together."

But Ringling Brothers, a mammoth operation with

nearly two thousand workers, proved daunting for Martha. She took Jenny back to Germany, leaving her daughter in the care of her mother so that she—Martha—could return to Karl in America.

"Mine was a disruptive childhood," says Jenny. "Yet I recall all these disruptions clearly. When I was three I came to America. I was told the move was permanent. In Sarasota, where all the circus performers lived during the winter, my father had one house with my mother Martha and another right next door with Helen. It was confusing. My mother acted as though he were still her husband—and he was, until 1934 when a telegram came from Mexico telling Martha that Karl had divorced her and married Helen. But that still wasn't enough to get my mother to leave the troupe. She sent me back to Germany under the care of my grandparents.

"When I was eleven, I visited my parents in Blackpool, England. Daddy had taken a leave from Ringling Brothers to tour Europe. I was finally reunited with my family. I was sure I would be with them forever. But then everything changed. The war was coming. And because Daddy, Helen, and my mother, Martha, had German passports, they saw themselves on the wrong side. They wanted to get back to America where Daddy saw his future. Europe was about to explode. Through Ambassador Joseph Kennedy, the future president's father, Daddy was able to get on one of the last boats. Three days later war broke out. But I didn't leave with them. By then I was back in Berlin with my grandparents.

"I remained in Berlin where I became a youth leader during the Nazi regime. I had no political feelings. I was simply a superb athlete, a young lady who did as I was told. I had no view of the larger world. By then my mother had married again, but that didn't last for more than a year. Six years—the war years—passed without a word from my parents. When Germany fell and the Red Army invaded Berlin, young girls were raped. I was among them. But not all the soldiers were brutes. Some were kind and compassionate. I fell in love with such a soldier. We were going to marry and then escape to America where I would finally join my parents. But his commanding officer discovered that he was involved with a German girl and he was sent to Siberia. I never saw him again. But I did, thank God, learn that my parents were alive and well. Daddy went to great lengths to secure my passage from Germany to join him and my mother, Martha, in Sarasota. I arrived in 1947, at age nineteen. Martha was still living next door to Karl and Helen. That strange triangle was still intact."

———

The world might have been falling apart around him, but during the war years in America Karl stayed focused. His artistry became more daring. He never stopped pushing the envelope. He began his decade-long plan to execute a seven-person pyramid, a stunt he saw as the most spectacular in circus history. His reputation grew and his troupe was called the Flying Wallendas. Ironically, he was quoted as saying that he never liked the name because, in his mind, it suggested that he and his troupe were flying off the wire in some disastrous fall, the fate that had befallen his brother Willy in Sweden. Willy's death was another reason Karl would not work with a safety net. Riding a bike across the wire, Willy fell, bounced from the net, and fractured his skull.

My great-grandmother Martha married for the third time. Her new husband, introduced to her by Karl, was J. Y. Henderson, the most celebrated veterinarian in the history of the circus. At the height of his career, he was in charge of Ringling Brothers and Barnum & Bailey's seven hundred animals—wildcats, bears, zebras, giraffes, antelopes, elephants, donkeys, buffalo, ponies, and horses. Not only did he devise innovative treatments to save the lives of hundreds of animals, he became a proficient wire-walker himself—a Renaissance man in the world of the circus.

In 1942, thirty-six of Doc Henderson's beloved animals died in a fire at the Ringling Brothers' circus in Cleveland.

In 1944, Karl and his troupe were on the high wire in Hartford when an even more terrifying fire broke out. They slid down the ropes and escaped through the animal chutes. In one of the most horrific events in circus history, 168 people died from asphyxiation.

Grandmother Jenny joined the troupe in 1947, the year she arrived in Sarasota. She became part of her father's treacherous and sensational seven-person pyramid, a high-wire stunt in which three ascending tiers of performers walked the wire, each linked by shoulder bars and poles. On the very top a woman sat in a chair carried by the two performers below her. Eventually Jenny became the woman in the chair.

She married Alberto Zoppe, a brilliant Italian bareback rider who had earned fabled status for his work with Circo

Italia, Circus Europa, and his own Circus Zoppe. In 1950 she gave birth to a son, Tino.

Meanwhile, Jenny had taken up her husband's specialty. She became so skilled that in Cecil B. DeMille's Academy Award–winning film, *The Greatest Show on Earth*, my grandmother was a featured bareback rider.

The same year the movie appeared—1952—Jenny's second child was born. This was Delilah, my beloved mother.

"For all his artistic genius," Jenny says of my grandfather Zoppe, "he was a violent and abusive man. There were times when I thought he would actually murder me. I had no choice but to divorce him. By then my father, Karl, had left Ringling Brothers and formed a troupe of his own. He was playing South America and asked me to join him. Whenever Daddy called me, I ran. I left Delilah in the care of my mother."

"My grandmother Martha," says my mother, "was the great religious influence in my life. I adored her. She had the heart and soul of a true Christian. Doc Henderson, her husband, was also a good and kind man, but it was my grandmother who demonstrated the love of God. She read me the Bible every night—not in a matter-of-fact way, but with great enthusiasm and passion. She took the time to explain the stories. She was careful to make sure that I knew that God cared for me, that God loved me, and that God would never leave me—no matter what.

"Those lessons were important because, while my mother was in South America, a man came to claim me whom I barely knew. This was my father, Alberto Zoppe. My brother Tino and I went to live with him. I was desperately unhappy. He was a man extremely interested in his son Tino. Tino's future as a performer meant the world to him. But this father had virtually no interest in his daughter. I felt terribly alone and afraid that my mother had abandoned me forever to a man who cared little for me."

Jenny returned from Karl's extended tour with a new husband, Dick Faughnan, a younger man whom Karl had trained to walk the wire. The raging battle between Jenny and Zoppe over their children continued. For long periods of time Jenny and Dick left my mother with relatives as they worked with Karl in circuses the world over. They became permanent parts of his seven-person pyramid—Jenny the slender woman on top. For my mother growing up was a time of uncertainty and confusion—and also excitement. She adored her grandfather Karl.

"It's difficult to describe the joy that he brought to people," my mother says. "He was born to entertain not only fans of the circus but his own family. He was a warm and loving man who kept us in stitches with practical jokes and silly pranks. He loved playing the clown and making children laugh. He loved life to the fullest. And while that family was fractured in so many ways, Karl had this amazing ability to bring us all together.

"At Christmas, I really could get myself to believe that we were one big happy family—my grandmother Martha, whom Karl had left for Helen; Helen and Carla, the daughter Helen had with Karl; Carla's son Ricky and daughter Rietta; Martha's husband Doc Henderson; Daddy's brother Herman; Herman's wife Edith and their son Gunther. There was also Marga, Karl's mistress. When Helen once left Karl, he took up with Marga. Helen returned, but Marga remained. Karl cared for Marga for the rest of her life and she became a part of the family.

"I know all this defies reason, but the Wallendas could hardly be described as reasonable. It might not have been reasonable for my mother and Carla to treat each other as full-blooded sisters, but they did. It might not have been reasonable for me to feel so much grandmotherly love for Helen, but I did.

"I was happiest when we were all together. During the holidays the old pains and betrayals were forgotten. There was a sense of solidarity. On any given evening, with the family gathered together, Karl could make us feel that everything was in order and the world was right."

My father, who became one of Karl's protégés, says, "He was a man who not only loved young people, but was a natural-born mentor. He was a phenomenal teacher. He had a passion for sharing the great skills he had developed over the years, and he did so with unusual patience.

"When it came to his competitors, however, he was unyielding. He would simply not be outdone. There were stories about him being on the road with various circuses and devising new stunts. He'd wake up in the middle of the night and practice on the high wire at 4:00 a.m. That way none of the other aerialists could get a glimpse of what he was doing. The man had an iron will and a fierce determination. He would not accept second place or second billing. He was also always looking to garner more attention by upping the ante. Above all, he was a competitive athlete."

"When I began performing as a young child," says my

mother, "that Wallenda competitive spirit entered into me. In the arena, there was this powerful sense of family solidarity. Like my mother and grandfather, I was becoming a wire-walker, and I loved every minute of it. I experience it on a very spiritual level. Not only was I walking in the literal footsteps of my elders, I was entering into that special place of quietude and serenity where I could feel the presence of God. To this day I cherish that place, just as I cherish God."

———

In 1962, the Wallendas were working for the Shrine Circus at the State Fair Coliseum in Detroit. My grandmother Jenny was about to be positioned on the top of the seven-person pyramid when her cousin Jana insisted that she take her place.

"My mother had a niece and nephew in East Berlin— Dieter and Jana—who managed to escape to America," says Jenny. "My father, who loved family, no matter how distant the relatives might be, took them in and trained them. I didn't think they were ready, but Daddy did. Jana wanted to take my place that night. I resented that. We had a big fight about it. She said, 'If you don't give me a chance tonight, I'll never get to do it.' I didn't want to, but I finally relented. I stayed on the platform as I watched the pyramid take form. Dieter, who was young and strong but looked unsure of himself, was the front man. The front man is the anchor. Daddy, his brother Herman, Herman's son Gunther, my husband Dick, and Daddy's adopted son Mario took their positions and began to move out on the wire. I wasn't worried about anything. Daddy had been performing this stunt since the forties and could do it in his sleep. I was still fuming that I wasn't part of it.

"As the three tiers of the pyramid took form with Jana seated in the chair on top, something suddenly went wrong. Dieter was losing control of the balance pole. I heard him cry out, 'I can't hold it any longer.' And right then, inches from where I stood, the pyramid collapsed. I watched it fall. It was the most horrible moment of my life. Dieter, Dick, and Mario were the first to fall. Daddy and Herman tumbled from the second tier but held on to the wire. Miraculously, Daddy grabbed Jana as she fell and held her hand until an emergency crew had time to run in with a net. Gunther was the only one who kept his balance and did his best to help Daddy and Herman. When it was over, my husband was dead. Dieter died as well. Mario was paralyzed for life. Daddy suffered a cracked pelvis and double hernia. The impossible had happened, the inconceivable, the worst thing in the history of the Wallendas."

The fall made headlines around the world. My mother, an eleven-year-old girl, was in Sarasota with Martha when someone called with the terrible news. Mom witnessed the women crying hysterically. Between sobs, they explained to her what had happened. Like her mother, she was incredulous. It couldn't be. The fall, the deaths.

Some called this the end of the Wallenda legacy. But on the very next night, at the same State Fair Coliseum in Detroit where the pyramid collapsed, Herman and Gunther were back on the high wire. Even more remarkably, Karl snuck out of the hospital and, despite his near-crippling injuries, hailed a cab and instructed the driver to take him to the circus. He changed into his costume and walked into the arena. A buzz went through the crowd.

Was this the man whose nephew and son-in-law were killed and whose son was paralyzed only twenty-four hours earlier, the same man who nearly lost his own life in the fatal fall?

He was announced over the public address system. "This is the great Karl Wallenda!" The ovation was thunderous. Despite the excruciating pain in his limbs, he climbed the rope, made it to the platform, and, his balancing pole firmly in hand, walked the wire.

His grief could not have been deeper, but his spirit was indomitable. His mantra remained unchanged: "Life is on the wire. Everything else is waiting."

To appease those family members who had been traumatized by the fall, he said that he would wait a very long while before deciding whether to perform the seven-person pyramid again. But the wait was no longer than a year. In 1963, at a circus in New Jersey, he did just that. He set the stunt back in motion.

In 1964, my teenaged mother became a full-fledged member of Karl's troupe, eventually sitting in the chair atop the pyramid.

In 1969, at age sixty-seven, Karl traveled to Georgia where he executed a spectacular walk across the Tallulah Gorge, a 750-foot-deep chasm covered with rugged boulders. In the middle of the wire, he stopped twice to do two handstands, a salute to the American soldiers risking their lives in Vietnam.

Over the years Mom was emotionally torn. Her mother

was distant. Her mother was working. Her mother was moody, obsessed with her own career, struggling with the same uncertainty that had preoccupied the Wallendas from the very beginning—financial survival in the precarious and brutally competitive world of circus entertainment.

By the time my mother met my father that world was on a dramatic decline. But they were kids and eager to meet all challenges. When they met in the early seventies Delilah Wallenda was twenty and Terry Troffer seventeen. Terry was still in high school. During the summers in Sarasota, he studied at Sailor's Circus, a training school where kids, hoping to become performers, learned the mechanics of putting up a tent and rigging the various stunts. He became a flying trapeze catcher. Fascinated with mechanics, a man of many talents, Dad showed unusual aptitude for the technical side of the circus. He also had gumption.

He knew that Karl Wallenda was among the world's most famous aerial performers and wondered what it would be like to work with the great man. The idea haunted him. But why would Karl Wallenda have any interest in a kid like Terry Troffer? Didn't matter. And besides, how do you get in touch with a Karl Wallenda? You look up his name in the phone book—which is just what my dad did.

"He was surprisingly accessible," says my father. "He liked training young people. He knew that if the circus had a future it was the hands of the young. He saw that I was eager and energetic. He hired me and a couple of other kids to work as flunkies on the road. We had to drive a truck and trailer to where he was performing in Clarksburg, Virginia. That's where I met Delilah. That's where my life changed."

My father broke his family's mold. His dad, a self-made man, began as an arborist whose passion was trimming trees. A savvy entrepreneur, he later began the Southern Waterproofing Company, which sealed, washed, and painted high-rises. While Terry ran off to join the circus, Terry's brothers became engineers with advanced degrees.

In 1974, Terry married Delilah.

"I trained him to walk the wire," says Mom. "Because I had been trained by the best—my grandfather and my mother—I understood that the key was overtraining. As a child of taskmasters, I became a tough taskmaster myself. The fact that my student was my husband made it doubly important that his training be uncompromised. If our dream were to come true—an act in which we would perform on the wire as a duo—then our lives would depend on each other.

"That meant Terry would have to be more than a competent performer. He would have to be superlative. He would have to be a Wallenda. I saw his other great talent was building and rigging. Like his dad and brothers, he has a supersharp scientific mind. But it was up to me to help him develop his talent as a performer. And he did."

The Delilah-Wallenda duo took shape. Mom and Dad became linked to the fate of her family. (When I began to perform as a child, I also adopted my mother's maiden name, knowing that "Wallenda" had both deep history and great mystique.) Karl hired them as members of his troupe. Terry rode a bike on the wire while Delilah, dangling from a strap attached from her neck to the bottom of the bike, was carried along.

"Karl was always happy to help family members hone their skills and develop their acts," said Dad. "There were two reasons. To begin with, that would mean that the family members were less dependent on him for support. He also understood the notion of expanding his brand. The more Wallendas out there, the better for the Wallenda name. That became especially important at a time when business had begun its steep downward curve."

As that curve sank even lower, the Wallendas faced fresh challenges. Fewer circuses were operating. Attendance was off. Money was sparse, but despite this Terry had embraced his wife's family creed. He and Delilah would make this thing work—no matter what.

Delilah's spirituality had a profound impact on Terry. Shortly after they married, he experienced an epiphany.

"It happened during a time when we were off the road," he remembered. "In order to make ends meet I was working for my dad washing windows. I was high up on a scaffold when I felt something with a power of its own come over me. Words can't explain it. I had been raised a Catholic, but never understood a church mass conducted entirely in Latin. I never had considered the Word of God, never really read it with anything approaching sincere concentration. But on this blazing hot afternoon, hanging fifteen stories above Sarasota, the sun in my face, I experienced what I'd have to describe as a miracle. I felt overwhelmed by a force that I can only describe as love. I found myself asking that source—whom I call God—into my life."

"When I picked Terry up from work that day, I knew he was a changed man," says Mom. "He had a smile on his face I had never seen before. He was radiant. Terry became a believer in a way that reinforced my own belief, studying the Bible and becoming not only a student of God's Word, but a scholar. He now knows God's Word as well as anyone I've ever met. Together we read David Wilkerson's *The Cross and the Switchblade*, a book about the miraculous impact of Christ on the lives of young people lost in gangs. We saw the movie. We discussed it in Christian study groups. In this critical period before beginning our family, we committed ourselves to the Christian life."

In 1977, Delilah gave birth to Lijana, my sister.

"It was beautiful to watch Karl respond to my daughter," says Mom. "He was a doting great-grandfather. In an instant, he switched roles from being a stern performer where no one or nothing could get it his way, to a softie. I treasure a photograph where Lijana, barely a toddler, is standing up in the palm of Karl's hand. He is teaching her balance. He just adored her."

At age seventy-three, Karl kept on keeping on. Two years before, his son-in-law Chico, climbing up to assist Karl on the wire, brushed against a live high-voltage clamp and fell to his death—still another tragedy to which Karl bore witness.

Yet no tragedy could stop him. Nothing could deter him from his work on the wire.

"One of his closest friends was Evel Knievel," says Dad. "The two men, bonded by their boldness, enjoyed a deep relationship. Neither knew the meaning of fear. And both had suffered a variety of mishaps. Both had persevered against overwhelming odds. You knew Evel was coming up the pathway to the house because you'd hear this loud clicking noise. This was the clicking from his broken bones. And yet, for all the pain, he was not a broken man. Neither was Karl. Until the very end, Karl stayed strong."

In 1978, at age seventy-three, he came to perform in San Juan, Puerto Rico. It was a hastily arranged engagement. His usual crew, back in Hawaii, was not able to do his rigging.

"Rigging," says my mother, "was the one thing my grandfather was absolutely adamant about. If he taught me and Terry anything, it was to trust rigging to one group and one group alone—your own personally trained crew."

Ticket sales to the circus event in Puerto Rico were drastically down. Always the go-getter, Karl decided to take matters in his own hands and stage a stunt to boost sales. He would walk 121 feet between the two ten-story towers of the Condado Plaza Hotel 121 feet above the pavement. In his long life, in a hundred countries and on five continents, he had done thousands upon thousands of such walks. His advanced age, his arthritis, and his double hernia were all challenges, but Karl Wallenda had faced challenges far more imposing. The San Juan walk was neither unusual nor especially spectacular. It was a mere publicity stunt to be covered live by the media.

My mother, back home in Sarasota, was recovering from a miscarriage, my dad by her side, when the phone rang. A frantic relative was telling them to turn on the television.

The scene was being replayed again and again.

Karl walked out on the wire. He was dressed in his usual white shirt and brown slacks. As always, he was composed.

He was a man renowned for balance. No one has been steadier, no one was more experienced, no one could even begin to approach his remarkable list of accomplishments. From the start of his six-decade career, he had been Mr. Calm, Cool, and Collected.

But this time something went terribly awry.

My folks' hearts started beating wildly. They could barely breathe. They couldn't believe their eyes. They saw that this man—their mentor, their teacher, the very paradigm of composure on the high wire, the great survivor of dozens of disasters—had lost his footing. He went to his knees. He grabbed the cable but couldn't hold on.

He tumbled through the air, landed on the concrete, and died instantly.

The television commentators called it the fault of a thirty-mile-an-hour wind.

"It's not the wind," said my father. "It's the rigging. I can see it from here. The rigging is wrong."

On that day everything was wrong.

Karl Wallenda, the mighty family patriarch, had fallen.

# 4

# A Kid in the Circus

Not only do most kids love the circus, millions of kids dream of being in the circus.

I'm a kid who doesn't need to dream. I'm actually *in* the circus. Unaware of any heavy family dramas that haunt my mother or the financial fears that plague my dad, count me among the happiest kids in America.

Here's how it works:

My grandfather, the dashing Alberto Zoppe, is thrilling the crowd with his daring bareback moves. He does pirouettes and cartwheels, handstands and backflips, all the while maintaining balance on the back of his white Arabian. He has the spectators in the palm of his hand. He approaches the crowd and asks for a volunteer. Everyone is reluctant. No one comes forward except this blond-haired little boy.

"Sure you're not scared?" asks Zoppe.

"No, I'm not scared," answers the kid.

Zoppe puts the kid behind him on the horse. As they go galloping off, the kid, his hands on Zoppe's shoulders, stands up. The kid removes his right hand from Zoppe's shoulder and waves to the crowd. The kid removes his left hand and does a little back flip. The crowd goes wild. For a few seconds, the kid is a star.

At the end of the stunt, Zoppe proudly introduces the kid as his grandson, Nikolas Wallenda.

I bow, hug my grandfather—who is one of my many marvelous teachers—and can't wait for the next show so I can do it all over again.

I know that my grandmother Jenny and Zoppe are no longer husband and wife, but have no knowledge about their violent relationship. All I know is that my grandfather is putting me in his act. He showers me with attention— far more attention, I will later learn, than he ever directed toward his daughter Delilah.

—

I make another appearance at Sea World in San Diego. This time, rather than playing the part of a stooge in the audience, I'm stuffed into a pillowcase. A clown flings me over his shoulder and carries me into the arena. He does his floppy routine. His baggy pants fall down to reveal pink polka-dotted boxer shorts. When he squeezes his nose, it sounds like a fire alarm. As he climbs on a unicycle and circles the arena, doves fly out of his pockets. At the end of his bike ride, the crowd is thoroughly delighted. It's time to bring their attention to the pillowcase. He reaches inside. The audience doesn't know what to expect—a baby bear? A lion cub?

He takes me by the scruff of the neck and presents me to the crowd. I'm a pint-size duplicate of him. I have the same makeup on my face, the same fire-engine-red bulbous nose, the same pink polka-dotted boxer shorts. He acts shocked.

I mimic everything he does: He does a pratfall, I do a pratfall; he does a somersault, I do two somersaults; he gets on his unicycle and tries to escape me; I have a miniature unicycle of my own and chase him all over the arena. He can't escape me. I am his mini-me and the audience can't get enough. When he stuffs me back in the pillowcase, I sneak back out. He doesn't see me but the audience does. I stand behind him where I mimic his every move. The audience howls. Mistakenly, he thinks the cheers are for him until he turns around and sees how his tiny double is stealing the show. He chases me around the arena but winds up falling on his face. I do a series of smart back flips and take my bow.

—

For the next ten years or so, I'm a clown. I relish the role. I love the persona. It's the foundation of my education as a performer. I couldn't ask for a better preparation.

The first—and most wonderful—fact is this: Being a clown is fun. It's not work. It's play. It sets up my understanding of circus stunts in terms of sheer enjoyment. It's a frolic, a romp, a game in which it's okay to play the part of a sad sack and loser.

Early on, though, I realize that the clown is also the character who has one purpose—to win your heart. The audience marvels at the daring of the trapeze artist or the courage of the wild animal trainer walking into the lions' cage, but it is the clown with whom they identify. That's because the clown is aspirational.

"Aspirational" isn't a word I know at age six, but I sure do have aspirations. That's why I'm a successful clown. The clown aspires to be in the show and will do anything, including falling on his face, to gain acceptance. The clown may act a little sad because others—in their form-fitting costumes and fancy plumage—are more glamorous and perhaps earn more respect. But the clown transforms sadness into joy by not taking himself seriously. The clown creates joy by making fun of his aspirations. The clown elicits your love.

The clown is also mute. He speaks with his body. His gags are visual, not verbal, but that makes it easy for a kid like me. There are no lines to memorize; no jokes to recite. The jokes are in the broad body gestures that dramatize my various dilemmas.

I work, for example, with the Cairn terriers that are part of my parents' troupe. I love these puppies. Clowns always need problems to solve, and the dogs provide me with a wealth of comical possibilities. I must get them to run through the hoops and leap over the little fences I've set up. One of the puppies runs astray and I must chase him down. When I do, another one falls out of line. The disorder continues. The crowd laughs at my efforts but also relates to my frustrations. At the end of my ordeal, I intentionally trip and land on my backside as all the puppies run over to lick my face before they run through the obstacle course. The kids in the audience love every minute of the act.

Kids are the easiest audience. Kids are also the purest audience. They are neither cynical nor critical. They are prepared to laugh. They want to be entertained on the simplest level. As a kid entertainer, I also have a pure heart. I want to do nothing more than delight the audience. This drive is inborn. My parents share the same drive—to please the people.

"They've worked hard, long hours all week long," I hear my father explain. "Many of them don't have it easy. They don't have a lot of money, so when they decide to buy a ticket to see us perform it's our job to make sure we give them a thrill. Same goes for the kids who've been cooped up in school. Everyone's looking for a little escape, Nik, everyone's looking to be amazed. It's our job to amaze them."

I love that job. It's a serious job that, for a kid, doesn't have to be serious at all. It just has to be about having fun and making sure everyone has fun along with me.

The serious part comes with my aspirations. Along with the audience, at every performance I watch my mom and dad. I marvel at their skills and yearn to do exactly what they're doing. They set up wires, only a few feet off the ground, that allow me to do just that. They encourage my aspirations. I have a ball clowning around, but I'm dead serious when it comes to perfecting my balance in what others might see as perilous situations. This want—you might even call it a compulsion—for serious fun continues for the rest of my life.

Before they go out to perform, I study my parents.

My mother is a beautiful woman with a sweet smile. She wears a fitted costume, a sparkly spangled outfit that is the aerialist's version of a one-piece bathing suit. My father is an imposing man in all respects. He has a muscular build, impressive upper-body strength, and a stoic demeanor. Together Mom and Dad are a handsome couple.

To my young eyes, they carry themselves with tremendous confidence. They display great showmanship and courage as they climb the ladder and walk the wire.

I see my sister following in their footsteps and have not the slightest doubt that I, too, will be joining them on high. It's only a question of time. I'm bursting with energy. I'm filled with purpose.

I do not expect that anything can or will go wrong.

Fear isn't a concept I understand. Fear isn't a feeling I've encountered. Fear has nothing to do with the universe that, as an overactive clown kid, I inhabit.

## 5

# A Kid Encounters Fear

I'm seven years old, sitting next to my sister at an airport in Puerto Rico. My parents are standing several feet away so we cannot hear their conversation. I know something's terribly wrong, though, because tears are streaming down my mother's face. Mom and Dad always try to keep strife and discord away from us, but, given the fact that we're a close-knit traveling family troupe, that's virtually impossible.

When they aren't looking, I inch a little closer so I can hear them speaking.

"It's impossible," says my mother. "It's useless. I can't go on like this."

"It's a bad break," my father agrees.

"All that work and the man stiffs us."

"I should have decked him," says my father.

"Thank God you didn't. The children don't need to see their father attacking a promoter."

"The man belongs behind bars."

"If only we had the money to hire a lawyer to put him behind bars," says Mom.

"How much do we have left?"

Mom rummages around her purse and finds her wallet. She counts the bills.

"Eighty dollars," she says.

"That's all the money we have in the world?"

"That's it."

Dad shakes his head in disbelief.

"Unbelievable."

"What are we going to do?" asks Mom in a voice filled with panic.

"I'm not sure," my father answers. "The situation keeps getting worse and worse."

"Well, at least our plane tickets are paid for."

For a long time my dad stays silent before my mom says, "Terry, I'm afraid."

"I understand, Delilah. Your fear is not unfounded."

This is the moment when fear is introduced into my consciousness. The fear has nothing to do with falling from the wire. It has nothing to do with perilous stunts or wild circus animals. The fear has everything to do with money. In my parents' faces I see the anxiety that comes with the most primal fear of all—*Can we survive?*

I hate that feeling of fear. I don't want to know it. I don't want to absorb it, but it enters my young understanding of the world. For the first time I learn that performing may not provide basic sustenance. This is a shock to me. I think of performing as the most wonderful thing in the world. How can performing not pay my parents enough money? They are great at what they do. Audiences love them. Crowds never fail to give them standing ovations. Shouldn't they get paid lots of money for doing that? After all, very few people have those skills. I don't understand how money can be a problem. I've spent time at the ticket booth where I've watched spectators hand over their cash. Where did all that money go? At least part of it has to be for my mother and father.

On the plane, I finally find the courage to voice my concern. I walk over to Dad, who's sitting next to Mom.

"Do we have enough money?" I ask him.

"What do you mean?"

"Are we all out of money?"

"Where'd you get that idea, Nik?"

"I saw Mom crying."

Mom, who has overheard me, says, "I was tired, honey. That's all. Everything is fine. Go back and sit with Lijana."

I take my seat next to my sister and decide to ask her about the situation.

"Why don't we have any money?"

"We have money," she says. "It's just that sometimes there's less money to pay the performers."

"Why?"

"Less people come to the shows."

"Don't they like the shows? I thought everyone likes the shows."

"Well, some people like to stay home and watch television."

"Our shows are better than television. Mom and Dad should get paid lots of money for putting on these shows."

"Eat your peanuts," says Lijana.

———

Back in Sarasota, after we unpack and rest up from the trip, I watch my father frantically make telephone call after call. He's desperate.

"Nothing to worry about," my mother assures me. She sees that I've picked up the worry vibe and does all she can to reassure me. But by now I have absorbed the emotional truth. I am aware that the danger does not come from any stunt that my folks practice in the backyard. The danger comes from the world itself. The world is not safe for performers like us because the world will not pay us enough to live.

From now on, I am aware of a new reality. Financial fear. The struggle to survive. The endless need to hustle up work.

At the same time I improve my skills on the wire. Every day I improve. Every day I practice. Every day I ask Mom and Dad to evaluate my progress. They are generous with their praise and exacting with their critiques. The older I get, the higher they raise the stakes—literally. The wire is always going up. Walking the wire becomes more comfortable for me than riding a bike. Soon, like my dad, I'm riding a bike across the wire.

—

It's a warm Sunday in Sarasota in early spring. Warm weather usually means more work. But it has been months since Mom and Dad have performed. Instead, they've been washing windows for my grandfather's company. They don't complain. They simply do it.

I practice all afternoon and well into the evening. After dinner, I'm exhausted and go to bed early. But sleep doesn't come. I hear the phone ring in the den.

"Pick it up, Terry," says Mom, who's in the kitchen, "maybe it's the agent."

An agent means work.

I crack open my door so I can hear my father's conversation.

"No," is all I hear him saying. "I won't do it. It's out of the question. I don't care how much money is involved. The answer is no!"

He slams down the phone.

"He wants us to play a carnival?" asks Mom.

"An entire carnival circuit," says Dad. "Six months of work—but the wrong kind of work."

I hear my mother sigh. "You did the right thing by saying no."

"Of course I did, Delilah. It's never going to happen."

In the coming years, I learn why. My parents say that the carnival is a shady operation. Con men are often in charge. The criminal element is strong. Drugs are everywhere, liquor is plentiful, and there's no way in the world they'll allow their children into that world.

"I'd rather starve," I hear my mother say.

Which makes me wonder—*will I?*

—

I wonder how much of my energy as a boy—and even as a man—is based on that psychological phenomenon that has me turning fear to energy.

I'm throwing three paper routes at once.

I'm mowing lawns like my life depends upon it.

I'm knocking on the doors of neighbors to see if they want me to trim their hedges and pull their weeds.

I'm doing all possible manual labor to earn extra change. I'm saving money with the idea that, if our funds are completely depleted, I can help my folks buy groceries.

These chores are accomplished without the slightest hint of resentment or regret. They're done with joy. I simply love to work. I can't work enough. I only wish that my parents could find work of their own. While my mother expresses hope, my dad's default position is despair.

"The money situation keeps getting worse," he tells Mom, thinking I'm out of earshot.

"It'll get better," she says.

"When?" he asks.

She doesn't answer.

Months pass without work.

I go to the Christian school attached to our church—the Tabernacle—where I'm an eager student. I like math and science. I'm fascinated by history. But it's the sacred studies I love most. The Bible stories come alive. I want to know how Moses will survive. How will Jacob ever get out of his jam? Even as a young boy, I understand that even those who love God struggle with survival. None of the Old Testament characters I like most have an easy time of it. Everyone has trouble. Everyone needs God. Everyone is on a great adventure. Reading the Bible, I can see these adventures on the movie screen of my mind. I'm amazed to see how some of the characters, like my father, fall into despair. Some, like Job, argue with God. Some, like Thomas, doubt Him. Others, like David, never stop loving Him.

At the Tabernacle Church, the Bible is taught as truth. My parents say the same thing. This is God's Word. I love that idea—that God is not only the all-mighty creator to whom we pray but also the author of stories that explain how He works in everyone's life.

In our life, when my parents finally find work, they are quick to thank God. With great joy and anticipation we pack our gear and hit the road.

When times are good, we can stay on the road for eight or nine months at a time. Mom becomes our homeschool teacher. She's stricter than our regular teacher, but Lijana and I don't mind. We're happy to be out there traveling the country and putting on shows.

Family unity is extreme. On the road we live, eat, sleep, drink, and stay together 24/7. We live in a thirty-one-foot trailer where there is no privacy. We have no choice but to be a high-functioning unit.

Essentially I grow up in an Airstream that my parents bought from Karl Wallenda in the midseventies. I love knowing that I am riding along in a vehicle owned by the man who visits my dreams. My parents tell me that most of the fairs and amusement parks where we appear are venues where Karl appeared as well.

Because there is no money for motels or hotels, the Airstream is our home. A couch opens up into a bed for Mom and Dad, and in the back Lijana and I each have a small bed of our own. Nothing fancy, but who needs fancy? When we're working, the energy is always up.

A box truck packed solid with all our gear pulls the Airstream up and down the highways of America. With Dad behind the wheel, Mom by his side, me and Lijana in the back, and our six Cairn terriers barking up a storm—jumping on my lap, licking my nose—we clock a thousand and one miles on a thousand and one days of my busy childhood.

The routine is rough on Dad. He has no assistant or hired hand.

—

We've taken three days to drive across the country—stopping only for bare necessities—when we finally arrive late in the afternoon at the fairgrounds in Sacramento, California. It's cold and rainy. Dad hasn't gotten much sleep because the truck broke down along the way. He was able to repair the engine himself, but the delay cost him four hours. The first show is tonight.

The second we arrive, I'm helping Dad unload gear. The show is outdoors—there's no tent—so with rain pouring down we find the area where Mom and Dad will be performing. I'm a strong nine-year-old but there's only so much I can carry. Dad has to haul the heavy platforms and two tall poles from which the cable will be strung. He has a twenty-pound sledgehammer to drive the iron stakes into the ground. I have my junior-size nine-pound sledgehammer and work right alongside him. We put the poles in place. We stretch and string the wire, making sure the tension is just right. Usually Mom and Dad rehearse before the show, but now there's no time.

I go on first. I've already changed into a red-and-white costume that Mom has made for me. She not only sews our costumes but hand-stitches our shoes. The crowd's already seated in the stands surrounding the high-wire platforms. Wearing my bright red rubber nose, I run out, carrying a picnic basket with one hand and pulling a little red wagon with another. One of the terriers, Apollonia, is in the basket while the others—Pepper, Zoobie, Toolie, Winston, and Shatzie—obediently sit in the wagon.

I spread a red-checkered tablecloth on the ground to prepare a picnic. As I bend over, though, Zoobie jumps out of the basket and hits me in the butt. I fall on my face. The crowd roars. When I get up to see what has happened, Zoobie has scurried back into the basket. I gesture to the audience as if to ask, "Who did it?" They point to the basket. But on my way to the basket the other five terriers leap out of the wagon and block my path. Winston is holding a rope in his mouth and drops it at my feet. I pick it up and do a highly coordinated jump-rope routine with the dogs that I've practiced for months. First it's me and Winston jumping together, then me and Winston and Pepper, until all the dogs join me. We're doing great, and the crowd is eating it up, when Zoobie jumps out of the basket again and gets under my feet. I'm back on my butt, entangled in the rope. The crowd is howling, the dogs forming a circle and racing around me. When I get up, all the terriers break into a precise military maneuver, dashing in and out between my legs. When I try to move away from them, they follow me, never breaking the pattern of their running course. Every once in a while—just for laughs—I get tripped up again, but the dogs never do. The dogs are the stars. I'm the clown, trying to keep up with animals a lot smarter than me.

Other animals are not only smart but dangerous. We all respect the fierceness of the tigers and lions and learn to keep our distance. But it's my mom and dad who teach me that the chimpanzees, thought to be so adorable, can be deadly to little kids. In fact, when we work in circus venues, my clown act often follows the chimps. My protective parents never allow me to wait in the wings as the chimps leave the arena. They don't want the chimps to see me, so they hide me in a basket until the troupe of monkeys has passed through. They don't trust their volatility. They've warned me never to look a chimp in the eye—that can set them off—and I've promised not to do so. There have been times when the chimps have attacked a small child for no apparent reason. I obey my parents' orders yet can't help poking my head out of the basket to sneak a peek as the squealing chimps run from the arena.

I'm also warned about elephants. My father tells me a story that confirms the power of their memory. A trainer who drank heavily abused them. He was fired. But on a certain day, a different man with alcohol on his breath got too close to the elephants. Remembering the smell of liquor, the elephants associated it with pain. One of the elephants grabbed the man with his trunk, dragged him into the cage, and, putting the great weight of its head on the man's chest, crushed him to death. It's a story I've never forgotten.

On our endless treks around the country I plead with my parents to tell me more stories. Fantastic tales of circus life—whether tragic or triumphant—always excite me. The tales also serve to break the boredom. The road is long and the box truck—stifling hot in summer and freezing in winter—is confining.

Mom makes sure that her kids never fail to do their homework. It's English grammar, mathematics, and science. Bible reading is mandatory. Dad tests us on our knowledge of Scripture and asks us to challenge him. No matter what passage I read from the Old or New Testament, he gives an exact citation.

"Other books are useful," he says. "Other books contain great beauty and wisdom. But this is the book where we see God's own story. This is the one where we feel His beating heart."

My heart is beating fast because on a busy interstate in Virginia, the truck has broken down again. An hour ago, Dad knew something was wrong, so he left the Airstream at a campsite where he and Mom had one of their hush-hush discussions. I knew it was about money. I knew that, once again, we were down to our last dollar.

Now Dad is trying to goose the engine.

"It's the fuel pump," he says. "The fuel pump is about to go."

Five minutes later, as we approach an imposing hill, the fuel pump goes.

"What now?" asks Mom.

"You gals get out," says Dad. "Nik and I are pushing."

I look at the road ahead. The steep incline is no laughing matter.

"Ready?" Dad asks.

"Ready," I confirm.

The two of us—with Dad doing a good 90 percent of the work—slowly, steadily, tenaciously stay at it until we push that thing to the top of the hill. At the bottom we see a gas station. I remember the hymn that says, "God will take care of you."

God takes care of my family throughout my childhood. God stays strong in my heart. God sings a song that I can hear deep in my soul, even—and especially—when my father voices discouragement.

"You see the glass half empty," Mom is always telling him.

"No, Delilah," he says, "I see the glass accurately. I don't pretend there is more water than exists. I deal in reality."

Dad's reality continues to be despair. Yet in the face of despair, he demonstrates fortitude. He sees his world dwindling, but he's not about to call it quits. I receive a mixed message: The future is seen through a prism of fear, yet the future must be faced with steely-eyed determination.

The Bible is always there. Mom is pointing out passages. Many of them sink in and stay for life:

Matthew 19:26: "Jesus looked at them and said, 'With man this is impossible, but with God all things are possible.'"

And 1 Corinthians 15:57: "Thanks be to God, who gives victory through our Lord Jesus Christ."

Whatever the circumstances, I feel blessed as a young boy. I feel blessed to have *Vati* Karl—Papa Karl, my beloved great-grandfather—march in and out of my dreams. When I finally hear about his death, I feel blessed that the story does not fill me with fear. It fills me with purpose. One day I will return to Puerto Rico and walk the wire where he fell. I believe my dad when he says it was not Karl's fault, but the fault of the rigger.

I feel blessed at Benson's Animal Farm in New Hampshire to befriend Boo-Boo the Bear. Boo-Boo is my pal. The cub and I go into the mountains where I pick blueberries for his lunch. Sometimes, in a playful mood, he knocks me over. He thinks I'm his brother. I think about the wondrous creatures created by God.

I see the most wondrous creature of all: a female.

I'm still a boy but I want to be a man. She's still a girl but she has the beauty of a woman. Her name is Erendira. She's part of the Vazquez family, a circus trapeze troupe. She, her sisters, and her parents are great performers. She does somersaults and handstands with an easy and gentle grace. I love her eyes, I love her smile. I want to speak with her, but, when it comes to girls, I'm shy. I want her to see my clown act—and I believe she does—but being a clown is hardly a way to attract a girl.

When I'm not in a clown's costume, I'm assisting my folks in their act. My outfit, hand-sewn by Mom, consists of little red shorts, a red-and-white striped shirt, and high white socks. I feel like a nerd. I am a nerd—a circus nerd.

Does Erendira even notice me?

When she smiles, I'm convinced that she's smiling in my direction, but I can't be sure.

"Just go over and talk to her," says a voice in my head.

"Don't be silly," says another voice. "You're not even a teenager. You have no business looking for a girlfriend. Stick to what you know. Put on your red rubber nose. Be a clown."

From time to time, at various venues from Florida to California, the Wallendas run into the Vazquez troupe. Like us, they're a multigenerational circus family with a long and rich history. My parents are friends with Erendira's folks. They often converse with one another at length. I want to speak to Erendira at length.

"They're having an even harder time than we are," Dad tells Mom. "Business is something awful. They're broke."

"Who isn't?" asks Mom.

I devise a plan—I will work extra hard, mowing grass and trimming hedges back in Sarasota, so I can save up money to help Erendira and her family. That will help me get her attention. That will get her to notice me and like me.

My sister Lijana sees that I'm smitten. "Just go over and start talking to her," she urges.

"I don't know what to say."

"Doesn't matter."

I don't move. I stay silent. Normally the most overactive boy anywhere, I find myself immobile and tongue-tied.

"I don't know what's wrong with me," I say.

"I do," says Lijana.

"What is it?"

"It's puppy love."

The words hit me hard. The words hit me as the absolute truth. I can't deny it. I can't help but think that, given my love-struck situation, I require a plan. I have none. But I do have a thought: If I'm going to attract a girl, this clown business has to stop—and soon.

# 6

# "Next Generation Wallenda Walks Wire for the First Time"

The newspaper, dated July 28, 1995, is from Old Forge, New York. The article says that at fifteen I'm making my debut at the Enchanted Forest/Water Safari. The article is not entirely accurate. I've been walking the high wire since I turned thirteen but, given the tradition of circus hyperbole, my folks make sure that I have several debuts in several cities. Early on I learn the importance of promotion.

The writer describes the event:

"During the family's performance Delilah Wallenda walked the wire and stood on her husband's shoulders as he stood on the wire, smiling at all times.

"She kept smiling as her daughter walked the wire and as her husband rode a bike back and forth on the wire.

"Nik walked up an inclined rope leading to the high wire. He did so without the aid of a balancing pole.... On the way up to the high wire, 20 to 25 feet above the ring, Nik lost his balance for a second or two and used his arms to steady himself. The eyes of 1,000 or more people were on him.

"My eyes were on his mother. She lost her smile when he lost his balance and got it back as quickly as he recovered.

"After the show, I asked Delilah how she rated her son's first ever performance.

" 'Very good,' she said. She was smiling even wider than before. 'I give him an A.'

"His father said, 'He's very talented and has courage and determination.' "

Then the writer quotes the promoter, who says, "Nik's a cocky kid. A typical teenager."

The promoter isn't entirely off base.

I am a little cocky. I know I have a natural ability and I'm eager to show it off. I'm not sure, though, how typical I am.

For example, that stumble described by the reporter is intentional. It's my way of involving the audience and adding drama—a way for them to root for me. If I appear more vulnerable, the emotional stakes are higher.

The black-and-white photo that accompanies the article shows a clear-eyed fresh-faced kid who has a passing resemblance to Howdy Doody, a comparison that does not thrill me. I want to be cool. The striking costume that Mom has made for me—with brightly beaded thunderbolts exploding on my matching vest and pants—is certainly cool. Yet there's no hiding my All-American innocence. I'm the red-headed kid next door, the paper boy, the eager beaver who bags your groceries at the supermarket and carries your bags to your car in the hopes of a fifty-cent tip.

My transition from boy to teen is a happy one. For all my love of clowning, I can't wait to retire the red rubber nose. It isn't that I don't appreciate the artistry of clowning. It's simply that the girls aren't going for Bozo. And more and more, girls are on my mind—especially one in particular.

—

I'm at the end of my clown period when I see her again. We're playing a music festival in Milwaukee when I notice that the Vazquez family is on the same bill. My heart skips a beat. I don't say anything to anyone—not even my sister. I don't want to admit how excited I am at the prospect of seeing Erendira again. I don't want to appear too eager, but I can't help walking the grounds in the hope of running into her.

After wandering around for a few minutes, I spot her. She's sitting on a bench, absorbed in a book. It's twilight and the colored lights of the nearby Ferris wheel cast her in a fairy-tale glow. I study for a long while. She is positively the most beautiful human being God has ever produced. I feel frozen, not simply by her beauty but by my own fear. I'm afraid of saying the wrong thing. I don't want to come on too strong and I don't want to come on too weak. I don't want to come on too needy and I don't want to come on too cocky. I don't have an opening line. I don't have any kind of approach. I don't want to interrupt her reading and I do want to interrupt her reading. I want her to pay attention to me—and not that book. But the book has her attention, and, as I swallow hard and make my way over to her, the book is the issue that I must address.

"Hi, Erendira. What are you reading?" is my pathetic opening line.

"Oh, hi, Nikolas. I saw that your family was performing here. I'm reading a romance."

Her answer leaves me tongue-tied. I don't know the first thing about romances.

"Is that like a long love story?" I ask.

"Yes."

"Well, I know some love stories in the Bible."

The minute those words come out of my mouth, I want to take them back. I sound like a nerd. I am a nerd. I love the Bible but this is hardly the time to bring up the Bible. The Bible, though, is the book I know best. If I'm going to get into a book discussion with someone, I'm most comfortable referring to the Bible. But who wants a book discussion? I just want to find a way to impress Erendira.

It isn't that she's cold or distant. She's a sweet and polite girl, but she doesn't really respond. I have the feeling that she just wants to get back to her book. I should let her, but something keeps me from moving. Something keeps me wanting to be in her presence.

"Mind if I sit down?" I ask.

"Of course not."

She goes back to her book. Good manners dictate that I stay silent. But I can't. I want to engage her in conversation.

"So there's this romance in the Bible between Jacob and Rachel." Erendira looks up from her book and says, "Oh."

"Yeah. It's in the Old Testament. You wanna hear the story?"

"Well, sure."

I'm not sure what I've gotten myself into. Does Erendira really want to hear it? And do I really want to tell it? Isn't my nerdiness getting out of hand? No matter, here I go . . .

"See, Jacob meets Rachel at the well and it's love at first sight."

As soon as I say those words—"love at first sight"—I blush. The words describe exactly what happened when, years before, I first saw Erendira.

"Do they live happily ever after?" asks Erendira.

"Not exactly. Rachel's father says that, before he gives his daughter's hand to Jacob, Jacob must work for him for seven years."

"That's a long time."

"Yeah, but the Bible says that Jacob loved Rachel so much that those years flew by in a flash."

"So they married after the seven years?"

"No—that's the sad part. Rachel's dad had another daughter—Leah. Leah was older than Rachel, and the father wanted to marry her off first. So he had the women put Leah in a wedding gown with a veil covering her face. Jacob thought Leah was Rachel. He got tricked into marrying the wrong sister."

"That's awful."

"Well, it gets a little better because in those days you could have more than one wife and Jacob said that he still wanted to marry Rachel. Rachel's dad said okay—if you work for me another seven years."

"And did Jacob agree?"

"Yes."

"And he married Rachel?"

"Yes."

"But I bet they didn't live happily ever after. I don't see how a man could be happy being married to two sisters."

"Especially since the sister he loved—Rachel—couldn't have children—and the other one—Leah—could."

"I don't remember any of the priests telling us stories like that."

"Priests?"

"We're Catholics."

"Oh. Do you like being Catholic?"

"Don't know anything else."

"Do you like performing with your family?"

"I love it. But I don't know anything else. How about you, Nikolas?"

"I love it, too. But now I love it even more."

"Why's that?"

"No more clowning. I've started walking the high wire."

"That's great."

"Will you come watch me?"

"Sure, if we're done with our show first."

"I'll come to your show. I always come to your show. I ..."

I'm about to say, "I always watch you. I can't keep my eyes off you. I want to be with you every minute of every day," but I don't. I keep what little cool I have left. I let Erendira go back to reading her romance, completely unsure whether she has the slightest interest in a romance that would involve me.

———

Romantic yearnings are pretty typical of teenagers. What may be more unusual, though, are my sleepless nights. For all my excitement about getting to perform on the wire, I'm experiencing heightened anxiety about the fate of my family's business.

Mom and Dad are in the kitchen. Their voices are low but the expressions on their face tell me the topic of conversation is money. We're low on funds. We're running out. Bookings are drying up. What can be done?

———

Mom and Dad are in the yard. They walk away from the house so I can't hear until my mother cries out, "Cancelled! That's impossible. He promised us we'd be working all summer. Now what are we going to do?"

———

Mom and Dad are leaving church. I'm a few steps behind. A friend of theirs approaches them with a warm greeting.

"We received a great Word today, didn't we, Terry?"

"We did indeed."

"How's work?"

"Slow," says Dad.

"Very slow," Mom adds.

"Sorry to hear that," says the friend. "But God's the great provider, isn't He?"

—

I believe in Jehovah Jireh, God my Provider. At no time in my life do I doubt the care of a God who loved mankind enough to sacrifice His son for the sake of our souls. His son lives in my heart. His son is the source of my strength. But my connection to the divine does not alleviate my anxiety about the earthly problems I see before me.

My passion is for performing. My passion is for walking the high wire. The figure of Karl Wallenda—in a dozen different forms—continues to populate my dreams. He is pushing me on. He is telling me that the tradition must be honored. There's nothing I want to do more than become an artist worthy of his name.

But all that's a dream. Cold reality is saying something else. Cold reality is saying that there's not enough work to sustain us.

My father is saying that.

My mother is saying that.

So night after night I stay up worrying. I don't admit this to anyone, but I often break into tears and cry like a baby. I cry because I'm scared we'll lose our house. I cry because I'm scared that we won't be hired by a single circus or amusement park. I cry because I'm scared that I won't get to do what I love doing most. I cry because I feel helpless over my fear. I cry because I have no control over the future—a future marked by uncertainty.

But come morning, I feel a surge of energy coursing through me. The energy has me up early and out on the streets. It's early June and the Florida sun is blazing hot. I take a bus to downtown Sarasota. I'm determined to get work. On the bus I remember how, years before, I worked hard selling concessions to the crowds while other acts were performing. I hawked popcorn and peanuts. I hustled hard, usually outselling the other vendors. People liked buying candy from this cute little kid. I'd come home with savings. Now I see that I need to add to those savings. I'm feeling that the only way to stop worrying about money is to make money.

I'm answering an ad at First Watch, a downtown restaurant. It says they need a dishwasher. I can wash dishes.

The manager is John Carson.

"Nik Wallenda," he says as he looks over my application. "The Wallenda family?"

"Yes, sir."

"Don't you work in your family's act?"

"I do."

"But you also want to work here?"

"Well, sir, the circus business is pretty slow right now."

"What about school?"

"I attend the Tabernacle church school, and we're off for the summer."

"When you do work with your family, what's your particular skill?"

"I walk the high wire."

"And a high-wire-walker like you has no compunctions about washing dishes?"

"None whatsoever, sir."

"And busing tables?"

"I'll be the quickest and best buser you've ever hired."

Mr. Carson laughed.

"So you're an eager beaver."

"Very eager."

"And when would you like to start, Nik?"

"Now."

"Now's as good as time as any. Follow me to the kitchen and I'll introduce you to Tony. He'll test your scrubbing skills in no time."

I pass the test with flying colors. I scrub, I rub, I scrape and rinse, I dry and stack the dishes with absolute focus. Within a few days, I'm a world-class dishwasher.

Mr. Carson takes notice. A week or two later, he calls me into his office.

"I'm impressed with you, Nik," he says. "When I hired you, I suspected you were one of those spoiled circus kids. But when I saw you mopping the kitchen floor without even being told to do so, I knew I was wrong. I want you out on the floor now. I want you busing tables. Are you ready?"

"I am. Sounds great."

It is great. I bus with such intensity that I do the work of two guys. I'm a dynamo, running around that restaurant and cleaning off tables like my life is on the line. It's easy and fun. I work five days a week, eight hours a day. Whenever I'm offered overtime, I grab it. Some weeks I work sixty or seventy hours. Those are my favorite weeks.

At the end of the summer, I have a mentor in John Carson.

"I know school's starting up, Nik, and I hope that you and your parents are able to get some bookings. I will never get in the way of that. But whenever you want extra work, just come down to First Watch and we'll find something for you to do."

"I want to keep working—even after school starts," I say. "I know I can do both."

"And how about your wire-walking?"

"Well, right now we don't have any engagements lined up, but if we do go out of town, the minute I get back I'll be down here doing whatever you need."

"I like your attitude, Nik."

"I like work."

I *love* work. Mere physical exertion keeps my head clear. I still have sleepless nights when I worry about my future as an aerial artist. Those are the nights when I start to see that I'll probably have to find another future with steadier work. I'm a realist and reality is telling me that I'll need a profession on the ground, not one up in the air.

I also derive great satisfaction from completing chores—especially those with monetary rewards. My formula is simple—turn my apprehension to energy. Rather than worry about the future, do something about it. While working, while engaged in intense physical labor—while busing tables, washing dishes, mopping floors, and mowing every lawn and trimming every hedge within three square miles of my parents' home—I'm relieved of anxiety. Anxiety may still be stirring somewhere deep down in my unconscious, but I'm sweating too profusely to realize it. The job before me has to get done. That's all that matters. The more strenuous the job, the happier I am.

And yet...

The dreams never stop.

In one, Karl Wallenda seems to be walking across the world.

"I want to walk across five continents," he tells me. "The wire will extend for thousands of miles. Watch me."

I stand below. High above me is not the old man I have seen in photos, but a young man in his thirties.

"Follow me," he says. "Get up here."

He extends his hand and suddenly his arm stretches hundreds of feet to reach me. He is a superhero capable of elongating his body. Each stride covers a mile. On the wire behind him, I find I can do the same. We are walking above the clouds, walking through mist and rain, walking with unshakable assurance that we will not and cannot fall. There is no fear, only joy. I look below and see the lights of magical cities. I look ahead and see the peaks of the snow-capped mountains. The wire tilts higher and we walk over those mountains. Day turns to night and the sky is lit by a yellow moon.

"We will walk to the moon," says Karl. "Are you ready?"

"I am."

"Follow me."

I follow. Now each stride covers five, ten, fifty miles. The pace quickens. We're no longer walking, but running. It's difficult keeping up with Karl, who has now aged into an older man. He is sixty or seventy. His face is lined and his gait not quite as steady.

"Do you need help?" I ask him.

"No," he says. "The Falls are on the other side of the moon. Once we reach the moon, you'll be able to cross the Falls. Are you ready to cross the Falls?"

"Yes!"

But in the yellow glow of the moon I lose sight of Karl. I keep running on the wire—faster and faster—but he is nowhere in sight. I run across the moon looking for my great-grandfather and see nothing but blinding yellow light. Then suddenly there it is:

Niagara Falls, in all its majestic beauty.

"Follow me," says Karl's voice. But where is he? Where has he gone?

I wake up, confused and excited.

The dreams come in a thousand different versions. Sometimes Karl is the central character and sometimes he is absent. But they all involve fantastic feats. They all involve wire and cable. They're all about walking over ragged rocks or roaring rivers or great gorges or canyons filled with fire.

No matter how many dishes I wash or tables I bus or lawns I mow, the dreams recur. My sleeping life feels as real as my waking life. Fantasy and reality clash.

I know what I want to do. I want to live my life on the wire. But I know what I have to do. I have to make money.

I pick up my Bible and turn to 1 Peter 5:7:

"Cast all your anxiety on Him because He cares for you."

I thank God for that caring.

I keep washing dishes, busing tables, mowing lawns, trimming hedges.

I keep dreaming dreams that every night become more vivid, more beautiful, more daring.

# 7

# Raising the Stakes

I'm at the Tabernacle church on a Sunday when I meet a new youth leader. His name is Chris Ripo. He's twenty-six, ten years older than me, and a lightning bolt of energy. He definitely loves the Lord, but isn't preachy or pedantic. He teaches Scripture in a way that challenges. He allows me to challenge him.

He quotes Philippians 4:9—"The things which you learned and received and heard and saw in me, these do, and the God of peace will be with you."

The key, according to Chris, is the practice—the acts, the actual work we do for God. Chris is all about action. He supports a Christian missionary charity that badly needs money and asks us church boys to help raise funds through manual labor.

Chris sees me as something of a cocky kid—a smart

aleck—and he's not wrong. He knows I'm a brash circus performer and he wonders just how much I'm going to be willing to get my hands dirty with hard labor. So he tests me. He gives me a job—strip a roof. That means removing the shingles and the sticky tarpaper beneath.

"How many guys you want up there to help you?" he asks.

"Don't need any," I say.

"You gonna do it all by yourself?"

"That's right."

"Well, I'll be back in a few hours. If you have half the shingles off by then, you'll be doing great."

When Chris returns, I have the entire roof stripped— every shingle, every last piece of tarpaper. The ground is littered with all the discarded materials that I've ripped off the roof.

"Wow!" is all Chris can say. "How many guys you get to help you?"

I just smile my wise-guy smile.

From then on, Chris and I are bonded. Along with John Carson, he becomes my mentor.

Just as John keeps promoting me at First Watch restaurant, Chris sees my never-say-die work ethic as close to his own. We are brothers in Christ, brothers in donating our time and energy to his missionary charity. Eventually we become business partners.

Chris is a man who works every legitimate business angle out there. He buys and sells cars. He teaches me to detail cars. He buys old houses and fixes them up. He teaches me to do everything involved in homebuilding and refurbishing. Before long I can do it all. I can lay the foundation. I can do the carpentry, the drywall, the plumbing, and the painting.

Chris and I have a spirited older brother/younger brother push-and-pull relationship. We wisecrack like crazy. For all the banter, though, there's a serious side to our relationship. Chris is the man who teaches me about fiscal responsibility. He teaches me the importance of savings.

Before meeting Chris I had already opened a savings account in my own name in which I put every spare dime I earned. Given my crazed compulsion to take all jobs that come my way—and to do those jobs quicker than anyone else—the money had started to add up.

John Carson rewards my initiative by making me an assistant manager at the First Watch restaurant. By then there is no job at the restaurant I can't do, from ordering the supplies to cooking the meals to training the waiters to making sure the steady customers feel at home.

When I'm not at First Watch, I'm with Chris Ripo, taking apart an old house or putting up a new one.

By age eighteen, I've saved enough money to buy my first car—a Nissan 240 SX. At the same time, Chris comes to me with a fascinating proposal.

"We've been fooling with construction for a while now, Nik," he says, "but how would you like to *buy* a house?"

"You already have a house, Chris. And my parents have theirs. What do I need a house for?"

"It's an investment. Real estate, bought cautiously, is always a solid investment."

I check my savings account. Amazingly, during my teen years I've been able to put away twenty-four thousand dollars.

"Take all my savings and put it in a house?" I asked Chris. "Isn't that kind of crazy?"

"It's the opposite of crazy. It's the sanest thing you can do. I'll put in the rest. We'll be partners in a rental property. It's a sound investment. Don't you see?"

I do see. I trust my brother in Christ. We buy the house. For years it provides the income that Chris promises. And we still own it today.

I'm not sure I know another eighteen-year-old who runs a major restaurant and also owns a house. Does this knowledge make me, as Chris might say, a little cocky?

The answer is yes, but under the cockiness there is also great conflict and fear. The conflict says, *You're a good moneymaker outside performing but performing is your passion.* The fear says, *You'll never get to pursue your passion.*

Then came the call.

—

"Who was on the phone?" Mom asked Dad.

"Your brother Tino. The Hamid-Morton Shrine Circus has been in touch with him."

"What does that have to do with us?"

"They want more than Tino. They want all of us. They want us to do the seven-person pyramid in Detroit. They want the setup exactly as it was back in '62."

"So it'll be in the same building?"

"Not only that, but the same area of the same building. They want the same style platform. The same everything. What do you think, Delilah?"

Mom is silent. The silence lasts longer than I can take.

"Let's do it!" I blurt out.

Startled by my remark, Mom and Dad both turn and look at me. Until now, they didn't know I've been listening.

"This is hardly your decision, Nik," says Dad.

More silence.

"I think Nik's right."

"You do?"

"I do, Terry."

"Yes!" I scream.

"Quiet," says my father. "This is a serious matter."

"I understand," I say. "But I'm ready."

"For what?" asks Dad.

"To do the pyramid," I answer.

More silence. The silence is driving me crazy. I wish they'd go ahead and say something.

"Well?" I ask.

"Well *what*?" says Dad.

"Don't you think I'm ready?" I ask.

All I get is more silence.

"I'm eighteen," I say. "I know I'm ready. I've been ready for years. You have to let me do it!"

"Your mother and I will discuss it," says Dad. "We'll let you know."

"You can't say no."

"I can say whatever I want. This is not a frivolous matter."

"I can do it."

"I know you can," says Mom.

"You need to be patient," says Dad.

"Can we start training today?" I ask. "Can we start right now?"

My father laughs. He knows there's no stopping me.

—

It's obvious why the circus has chosen Detroit to re-create the pyramid. Detroit's the scene of the fall. Doing it in Detroit will create maximum drama and maximum publicity. In Wallenda lore, Detroit is associated with tragedy. Now tragedy must be turned to triumph. I want to be part of the transformation. I want to make it happen.

The call comes in the fall of 1997. The actual event is slated for March 1998. We rehearse in our backyard for six months.

The training is intense. The pyramid is a delicate operation. There can be no doubts, no hesitancies, no missed cues. Coolness and calm confidence are the order of the day.

On the first day, I'm out in the backyard a full hour before anyone else arrives. As I set up the platform, I feel myself stepping into family history. Now I am part of changing that history. I can turn a negative to a positive. I can help lift that darkness that has hung over us for so long.

Just as I step out on the wire for a practice walk, I spot my uncle Mario approaching in his wheelchair. This is my grandmother's adopted brother, who was part of the pyramid that collapsed, leaving him paralyzed from the waist down.

"Hey, Nik, let me see you do that headstand," he says.

I'm happy to do it. It's Uncle Mario who first taught me to do the headstand on the wire. When he was still performing, the headstand was his specialty. I wasn't much older than thirteen when Mario came over, rolling his chair right next to the wire, and instructed me on how to handle the balancing pole while turning my body upside down. He taught me the headstand, step by step. He called me his favorite student.

"So I heard the news, Nik," he says.

"About the pyramid?"

"Yes."

"Isn't it great, Uncle Mario?"

"Do you know how old I was when the pyramid came down in Detroit?"

"No."

"Your age exactly."

His reply stops me in my tracks.

"Don't stop," he says. "Go ahead and do the headstand."

I do it.

"Perfect," he says. "But a headstand requires no one's skill other than your own. The pyramid is different."

My uncle is no one I wish to challenge. I have great respect for the man. I love him deeply. But as I step off the wire and look into his eyes, I see three decades of frustration. The pyramid crushed not only his body but his hopes and dreams. There is no crueler fate for an aerialist than to be confined to a wheelchair. It is his prison. So I understand what he is seeing and what he is saying. He's seeing himself in me. He doesn't want to see my hopes and dreams destroyed. The caution he's expressing is coming from a place of love.

How can I respond?

I don't.

"I understand, Uncle Mario," is all I can say.

"Do you really, Nik?"

"I think I do."

"All I'm saying is that I wish your uncle Tino and your parents would change their minds. I don't believe this is a good idea."

I have no response. At the same time, my determination to accomplish this feat is not diminished. My determination is stronger than ever.

Uncle Mario stays that day to watch us train. He returns the following day and every day thereafter. His presence is powerful. As he watches us from his wheelchair, I can feel his steely gaze. And although he may be looking on with a degree of disapproval—wishing that we wouldn't tempt fate—I don't take it that way. I prefer to absorb his energy as something positive. I see him as a man who, despite his bitter history, has loved me enough to become one of my devoted teachers. If I do anything wrong in this pyramid, no matter how subtle, Uncle Mario will point it out. I see his presence as a comfort.

The training goes well. The four anchormen forming the base of the pyramid—my dad, my uncles Tino and Sacha, and I—are steady and strong. Cousin Alida and Tony Hernandez, who has since married my sister, Lijana, are superb. Seated on a chair atop the pyramid, Mom is the consummate professional. During rehearsals, when we are only a few feet off the ground, there are no slip-ups. As we move to the regulation height, the formation never falters. It's beautiful to be part of such precision.

The re-creation of the pyramid comes at an especially

critical moment in my life. About to graduate high school, I'm facing a major decision—what to do next. Before this Detroit booking comes along, the aerial business for Mom and Dad is agonizingly slow. They have to depend on their other jobs—Mom is a hostess at a country club restaurant, Dad a union-member carpenter.

They are not encouraging me to carry on the tradition—not because they don't love it but because in all good conscience they don't see it sustaining me.

John Carson is telling me that, whether I go to college or not, I have a future at First Watch.

In addition to his many business activities, Chris Ripo has become a fireman and is encouraging me to do the same. The salary is good and the benefits excellent. What do I think?

I think that I want to go to Southeastern University in Lakeland, Florida, a great Bible college. What could be better than pursuing a serious study of God's Word?

I think that eventually I want to go to medical school and become a pediatrician. What could be better than promoting the health and healing of the very young?

All these ideas are great. I know that being a Bible scholar and a baby doctor are wonderful pursuits. At the same time, my first love is the wire. But the wire equals being broke. Or does it?

The press excitement surrounding the re-creation of the pyramid begins to build. The hype comes fast and furiously.

When we get to Detroit, there are a dozen media trucks. *Entertainment Tonight. Larry King Live. Hard Copy. Extra.* CNN.

Uncle Mario has come to watch the event.

"They're here to see if history will repeat itself," he says. "They're here hoping for another tragedy."

I don't view it that way. I'm thinking that if the Wallendas can generate such widespread publicity, why have my parents been struggling so hard and long to get work? Why should the Wallenda brand be dying when, with the right event, the Wallenda name can excite this much interest?

Maybe there *is* a career here after all. Given the right approach, maybe there's a way to regenerate Karl's tireless drive to keep himself in the public eye.

The public loves the idea of this Detroit re-creation. They love the story behind it—that thirty-six years later the same family has returned to rewrite their own history.

On the night of the event, I feel no tension. I see Uncle Mario watching—he's always watching—and thank God for his presence. On a spiritual level, we're doing this to honor his sacrifice.

We're doing this to display courage and confirm the continuity of a tradition that began hundreds of years before I was born. We're doing this without fear or apprehension. We're doing this as professional performers whose mission is to entertain and thrill the audience.

I'm thrilled to see the enormous press coverage. It seems like a thousand cameras are aimed in our direction.

The seven of us are standing proudly on the platform.

I walk out first and put the bar on my shoulders.

Standing on the platform, Dad puts that same bar on his shoulder before our cousin Alida stands atop it.

The first three-person pyramid steps out onto the wire.

In the same fashion, Uncle Tino and Sacha, with a bar on their shoulders supporting a standing Tony, create the same configuration.

A six-person pyramid has now been formed

Atop the bar supported by Alida and Tony a chair is put in place. My mother, seated in that chair, becomes the seventh person.

We're ready to roll. We wait a few seconds so the audience can cherish the drama. Now we slowly start to move. Before we do, though, a slight slump from one of the men on the bottom tier causes a horizontal wave of motion that moves across the pyramid. To keep this remarkable human structure from collapsing we all must move with the wave. Then comes another wave—this one coming from someone on a higher tier who has lost a bit of balance. This wave moves vertically, from top to bottom.

Rather than fight the waves, we must move with them— side to side, up and down. We must let them ever-so-slightly bend us without breaking us.

Finally, all seven of us, our long balancing poles undulating, are slowly moving across the wire. Halfway across, we stop in our tracks. That's when Mom stands in the seat of her chair and lifts her balancing pole above her head. The audience gasps. The symmetry of the seven-person pyramid is perfection itself. Mom sits down, and, after a few more seconds, we walk across the wire. The walking pyramid is poetry in motion. Every member of the audience—every man, woman, and child—holds their breath. The whole operation takes no more than four minutes—four minutes that many of the spectators will remember for the rest of their lives.

One by one we step off the wire onto the platform and slowly disassemble the pyramid. When the last man has reached safety, we extend our arms to mark our triumph. The crowd roars.

We've redeemed history.

We repeat the stunt thirty-eight times in the next seventeen days.

We leave Detroit as heroes.

I can't deny it; I love heroics; I love doing what everyone warns me against doing.

At the end of the engagement I see Uncle Mario wheeling himself into the dining area where the performers congregate after the show.

"Well, Nik," he says. "You paid no attention to me."

"Not true, Uncle Mario, I always pay attention to you."

"No, you ignored my warnings. You did as you pleased."

"But aren't you pleased, Uncle Mario?"

He pauses. His eyes are teary. He's too choked up to speak. He nods his head and is finally able to say a single word.

"Yes."

# 8

# Dinner and a Movie

I saw where your family re-created the seven-person pyramid," says Erendira.

"We did."

"I think that's great."

"Thanks."

We're at a circus in Sarasota where we've both just performed. I haven't seen Erendira in several months. I wrote her a note but never heard back. That broke my heart. I figured I didn't have a chance. But now she's being nice to me. I don't know what's going on.

"I wrote you a letter," I said.

"You did? I never got it. Where'd you send it?"

"Your home address."

"Well, you know we're never home. What did you write about?"

"Nothing in particular. Just wanted to know how you were doing."

"That was sweet of you. How are *you* doing?"

"Okay."

"I hear you have a girlfriend," Erendira says.

"What! Where'd you hear that?"

"Word gets around. Is it serious?"

"It was over before it started. She wasn't even a girlfriend. Just someone I dated a couple of times. It happened after I never heard back from you."

"Wait a minute, Nik. You're telling me that if I'd seen and answered your letter, you'd have never asked out that other girl."

"Maybe."

"There's a smile on your face. Does that mean you're lying?"

"No, it means I'm happy to see you. How about dinner and a movie tomorrow night?"

"Sure."

I'm sure about Erendira. I've been sure about her since we met as kids. She's beautiful, smart, and talented. She has a fiery spirit and a sparkling personality. She understands the life I lead—and want to lead—because she's been living the same life.

The next night we go to a little Mexican restaurant. We discuss everything. She's the kind of woman who's easy to talk to. She doesn't criticize or judge. She gets me. She feels the depth of my financial fears because she has them herself. She tells me how her family, for all its artistic brilliance and proud history, has gone through the same thing.

If anything, their economic desperation has been worse than ours. Over the years, they've nearly starved. Erendira talks about living for a whole week on nothing but rice and ketchup. Yet the Vazquez crew, like the Wallendas, have not given up. They continue to pursue their craft.

Erendira's life has not been easy. Her father has not been loyal to her mother—to say the least. The fact has made her suspicious of men. She isn't sure she could ever fully trust a man.

"You can trust me," I say.

"How can I know?" she asks.

"Listen to your heart."

"I think you've given your heart away to more than one girl," she says.

"I haven't. I promise."

"It's easy to promise."

"But what I'm about tell you isn't easy to say. Most guys would never admit it."

"Admit what?" she asks.

"That I'm a virgin."

My confession hangs out there. Erendira considers my words carefully.

"Is that something you're proud of or ashamed of?" she asks.

"Proud."

"So you're saying that you've just been too shy or that you've been saving yourself for the right woman?"

"I'm saying that, for me, sex is something to be cherished in the intimacy of a committed relationship."

"I don't know how to take this all."

"I'm just being honest, Erendira. I'm just saying that I believe in God and God's morality."

"You talk like you're older than you are."

"My best friends are all ten years older than me," I say. "My mentors are family men who lead exemplary lives. I want to follow in their footsteps. They're happy, productive, and filled with ambition."

"And what are you ambitious for?"

"Happiness, a family, and a career as a performer."

"Given what both our families have gone through, you don't think that's a pipe dream?"

"I don't think it's easy, but I'm not the kind of guy who gives up. Ever. I want to build up the Wallenda brand. I want to bring it back to where it was when my great-grandfather was at his height. And then go up from there."

"Other Wallendas have tried to do that," says Erendira. "There are a lot of Wallendas flying around the circuit."

"But there's only one Nik Wallenda," I say.

Erendira can't help but smile.

"I know that sounds boastful," I say, "and I don't mean to brag. I respect all my relatives' talents. They're great. But they haven't been great businessmen. I've been trained by amazing businessmen like John Carson and Chris Ripo, guys who have taught me the importance of entrepreneurial invention."

"Doesn't sound like you have doubts about anything, Nik."

"I have lots of doubts. But I'm not going to let any of them get in my way. I'm going to do what I know Karl Wallenda would want me to do. I'm going to do things no one else has ever done."

"Well, I know what you should do right now."

"What's that?"

"Eat your enchiladas."

———

During the movie, I reach over and hold Erendira's hand. She allows me. The touch of her soft skin is heaven.

During the ride home, she takes my hand.

When I walk her to the door of her parents' home, I lean over and kiss her on the cheek. She turns and lets me kiss her on the lips. We embrace.

I am dizzy with the excitement of being absolutely in love with this woman.

———

December 19, 1999, five weeks away from my twenty-first birthday.

My family is performing the seven-person pyramid at the Molson Center in Montreal, Canada. The Vazquez family is also on the bill. Early in the morning, I make it a point to seek out Erendira.

"Will you come to see us tonight?" I ask.

"I'd rather not."

"Why?"

"Well, I see that you and your brother-in-law aren't getting along."

Tony, my sister's husband, and I have some issues.

"When it comes to the act itself, that won't make any difference," I say.

"I'll be nervous watching," says Erendira.

"When we get up there, we put all differences aside. Same as your family does."

"But still…"

"You have to come, Erendira. You have to watch us. I'll be miserable if you don't."

"If you insist."

"I do."

That evening when we seven climb up to the platform I look down to make sure Erendira is watching. She is. My heart is racing.

We execute the pyramid flawlessly. The crowd rewards us with a standing ovation. The other six climb down from the platform but I remain. To the audience's surprise, I walk back out on the wire.

At the same time, my uncle Giovanni asks Erendira to walk to the center of the ring below. She doesn't understand why—and refuses. It's circus tradition that no one who is not performing steps into the center ring. But Uncle Giovanni is insistent. He gently but firmly pushes Erendira into the ring.

That's when I walk to the center of the wire and go down on one knee, my eyes fixed on Erendira.

I speak into a wireless mic so every last member of the huge audience can hear. My voice rings out with conviction.

"Erendira," I say, "I love you very much and I want to know if you'll be my wife."

I can see shock in Erendira's eyes. She's flabbergasted, totally taken by surprise. No sound comes out of her mouth.

My mother comes up behind her and whispers in her ear. "This is the part when you're supposed to say 'yes,' my dear."

"Yes!" she says.

The crowd explodes with thunderous applause.

I run off the wire, scramble down the rope, and run into the arms of sweet Erendira.

We embrace.

It's against my principles to live together without being married, so a week later, lacking the funds to rent a hall and throw a splashy party, we have a simple courthouse ceremony.

God is present. He is always present. The God of undying love is present when we take our vows. Before God, we commit our lives to each other. Before God, I feel a happiness, a glow of boundless joy.

I thank God for Erendira. I thank Him for changing my life in a new and wholly positive direction.

Huge challenges await us as a couple. There will be valleys to cross and mountains to climb. We will stumble and, at key points, we will fall. Our relationship will be challenged in critical and near-fatal ways. But on January 3, 2000, the day of our wedding, I can see only a future filled with bliss.

I've married the woman of my dreams.

## 9

# New Family First

Six months after the birth of our first son, Yanni—another one of God's miraculous blessings—Erendira is ready to return to performing. Because of financial constraints, we're living with my parents. These same constraints have kept me working at the First Watch restaurant forty hours a week in addition to whatever occasional bookings we can get. As usual, money is tight and tensions high.

I love my wife, I love my son, I love my new family, yet this love only makes me want me to do bigger and greater things.

"I'm with you," says Erendira. "I want us to perform as husband and wife."

There's nothing I want more.

"Be careful," says my father. "The market is dwindling. I don't see it getting any better. Plus other Wallendas are out there pushing their brands."

"They can be more than simply competitive," adds Mom. "They can be vicious. I hate to say this about my own relatives, but I know them well. They're my blood. And in our family history, there's bad blood everywhere you look."

I know the history. Karl Wallenda still makes periodic appearances in my dreams. He still urges me on, leading me through jungles and forests to where waterfalls converge and voices urge me to cross over valleys of fire. But I also know that 1 John 4:18 says that a perfect love casts out fear. I'm looking to perfect that love—love of God, my wife, my son, and yes, even those members of my extended family who might wish me well.

My spiritual mission is simple—stay focused on the positive. Avoid the toxic energy field of negativity.

My professional goal is equally simple—hone my craft so that I can provide for my family doing what both my wife and I love best.

Through my work with John Carson and Chris Ripo, I've been an entrepreneur in training—hungry to build my own brand.

"Do you think we can do it?" asks Erendira, whose family history of financial failure is nothing she can ever forget.

"I *know* we can," I say.

"Where do we start?"

"Kinko's."

Like thousands of would-be small business people before us, we run over to Kinko's, where I make my first brochure touting this new husband-and-wife team—the Wallenda Family.

The brochure is awful. My graphics are hokey, my wording is awkward, and the advertisement is hardly representative of what I consider a class act.

"This won't attract anyone," says my father. "It looks amateurish."

He's right, but given my limited skill as a designer of promotional materials, it's the best I can do.

I mail it out to key agents and venues where I've worked as a kid. After a week, no response. Two weeks go by and still no action. By the end of the fourth week, I'm starting to think that Dad's right. This new venture featuring me and Erendira is a lost cause.

And then comes a call.

I remember an old lady in church saying that you may not think God is there when you want Him, but He's always right on time.

This call is right on time.

"There's a Japanese promoter looking for something spectacular," says my father-in-law. "You're always thinking spectacular. Maybe you should call him."

"I will."

I do.

"We're looking for something spectacular," says the man, who books Tivoli amusement park in Kurashiki, Japan.

"I've got something spectacular," I say.

"What is it?"

"My wife and I have an amazing act on sway poles."

"Not spectacular enough."

"I ride a motorcycle across the wire."

"Not spectacular enough."

"What do you want?" I ask.

"Something that will make news. News will draw crowds."

"Like doing something that's never been done before?"

"Now you're talking."

I think for a few seconds. Then the idea pops into my mind.

"How about if I set a world record?"

"That can work. What do you have in mind?"

"The Wallendas are famous for the seven-person pyramid, but no one has ever mounted a four-layer *eight*-person pyramid before a live audience."

"And you can do that?"

"I can," I say, "and I will."

"I've very interested in this idea. We can promote it heavily. *For the first time anywhere in the world, a four-layer eight-person pyramid—exclusively at Tivoli in Kurashiki!* But you're certain you can do this?"

"Positive."

"Then it's only a question of working out the financial details. Should I contact your agent or manager?"

"You're talking to my agent and my manager."

"I'd want to book for at least six weeks."

"Six weeks would be great."

"I wouldn't want the eight-person pyramid to be executed until the beginning of the fourth week. I'd want to build up the excitement—and then set the record. Would the *Guinness Book* recognize this feat?"

"They'd have to."

"All that would have to be arranged in advance—or else no deal. What kind of fee are we talking about?" he asks.

I didn't expect things to go this quickly, so I ask if I can back get to him.

"No later than tomorrow," he says.

I discuss the matter with my father.

"I'd be careful, Nik," he says. "I'm not sure these people will pay you what you want."

"Well, all I can do is ask."

"You're going to have to bring your crew," says Dad. "You're going to need at least a dozen people to go over there with you."

"I figure I'll need at least fourteen."

"That will cost you a fortune."

"I'm going to ask a big fee."

"How big?"

"Two hundred thousand."

"You're dreaming, son. Tivoli won't pay that."

"Can't hurt to ask."

"I just don't want you to be disappointed."

The next day I call the booking manager.

"How much?" he wants to know.

I take a deep breath and begin to say the words. Those words won't come out. So I take an even deeper breath and finally say, "Two hundred thousand dollars for six weeks."

"And how much would you require up front?"

"Half."

"I'll go with your fee but can't pay more than a third up front. What do you say?"

"I say you have a deal."

When I tell Dad, he's still skeptical. "And what if you never see the remaining two-thirds of your money, Nik? What will you do then?"

I have no answer for my dad. I'm too excited to argue. After all, this is the first deal I've made on my own. I'm not thinking that the promoter would ever cheat me. I'm just thinking of setting my first world record.

When the contract arrives, I'm still in a state of semishock. I've cut my first deal. I'm about to execute my first contract as an independent artist. When I sign my name on the bottom line, I realize that nothing will ever be the same again.

There's no going back. Just like that, at age twenty-one, I'm in charge of a troupe training to break my own family's world record.

My mother is an intense trainer who trained my dad, who became even more intense than his teacher/wife. Rigorous training is my birthright and I probably take it further than both my parents put together. I am unrelenting. Because this is the first step into the big time out on my own, there can be no mistakes. I realize that not everyone will be rooting for me. What I'm doing, especially at so young an age, is unprecedented and audacious. If I trip up, my brand will be tarnished—perhaps permanently.

To help boost my confidence even further, I ask my parents to join me. I'd like Mom to stand atop the pyramid. I'd like Dad to be there for training and support. My request catches them by surprise. This represents a reversal of roles. Now they'll be working for me. Are they willing?

"You're our son," says Mom, "and we'll do anything we can to help you. We'll be there."

I want Mom's brother, Uncle Tino—a man I've deeply admired my entire life—to join me. He agrees but then changes his mind. He doesn't like the fact that I, and not he, have booked the engagement. Understandably, he views himself as a family patriarch. He can't see himself answering to his upstart nephew.

My troupe is nonetheless solid. My wife and partner, Erendira, is with me every step of the way. Her dad agrees to join us. We also have sister Lijana there along with her husband. Tim Carlson, a great performer and friend, is in. And then there's Mike Duff, one of my best buddies.

I've known Mike since kindergarten. When we played as kids, I showed him how to walk the wire in our backyard. He also studied at Sailor Circus, the same training facility where my father learned his craft. Mike's a natural. Plus he's all heart. His presence comforts me enormously.

I know I'm ready to break out. But the naysayers keep asking the question—some to my face, some behind my back—"Hasn't Nik bitten off more than he can chew?"

My answer is short and sweet. My answer is Philippians 4:13: "All things are possible through Christ Jesus."

No, I don't believe that God's invisible hand is holding me up on the wire. And no, I don't believe that God's intervention will keep the eight-person pyramid from falling. But yes, I do believe that I am strengthened by the steadiness of my faith. I do believe in a God whose steady love is unshakable and eternal. That belief allows me to get beyond my apprehensions and ignore what otherwise might feel like my limitations.

"Most people work at a fraction of their potential," says my mentor Chris Ripo. "Even hard workers like you and I might be utilizing 20 or 30 percent of our potential. That means there's still another 70 percent of untapped territory."

That idea excites me. It convinces me that, despite the negative voices, I am not taking on more than I can handle. I'm just moving into untapped territory.

It's not that I can eliminate all doubts. I worry that perfecting this operation—a huge one for me—might take longer than I had anticipated. But that only makes me double down on the work.

During training, I can lose my temper—always a problem for me. I can be short with my colleagues. As a boss, I can be overly demanding. Patience is not one of my strengths. Impatience doesn't always endear me to others. I am so single-mindedly goal-oriented that, in pursuit of that goal, I can ignore other people's feelings and emotional needs. That includes my wife. But at this point in my young life, when I'm so close to a daring feat that will put my name on the map, psychological niceties are not my concern. I want to make it. I want the world to know—the world to see—that the Wallenda family, the *Nik* Wallenda family, is expanding the tradition of the great Karl Wallenda. We're going all out to thrill audiences in new and spectacular ways.

I put together a full spectrum of entertainment. My sister performs a slide for life—a huge incline at the end of which she hangs by her ankle. Erendira and her dad perform the revolving perch: A motorized rotating pole emerges from a twenty-foot base. As it spins, he hangs by his ankles and picks up his daughter. She initiates a series of graceful poses and bodily configurations. At one point Erendira and her dad, without the use of their hands, connect neck to neck. In another stunt, my wife climbs one enormous sway pole while I climb another. At the very top, we execute all sorts of gyrating maneuvers before she leaps to my pole as I leap to hers. The culmination of our show is the seven-person pyramid. We will do it for the first three weeks. At the start of the fourth week we will—for one time only—add the eighth person and break the record.

In our backyard in Sarasota we practice every day. We start at ten feet up, then move to fifteen, then twenty-five. We practice our moves over and over and over again. We build up to the point where we stay on the wire for fifteen minutes at a time. Then we put another member on our shoulders and, supporting that weight, remain on the wire. We support the weight for four minutes, then ten, and finally a full fifteen.

The three-person pyramid becomes a four-person pyramid, then five, then six, then seven until we eventually reach eight. At each stage, we slowly and carefully perfect our moves. There is no rushing. Steady practice is the key.

Just as steadily, the promoter in Japan is preparing the press. The promotional buildup parallels our training. International news outlets are alerted. Interviews are arranged. Live coverage is secured.

The first three weeks go off without a hitch. Japanese audiences crowd the venue and love our show. The seven-person pyramid tops off each performance as the promoter saturates the market with news bits about the upcoming record-shattering spectacle.

And then comes the day of days: For the first time in world history, the eight-person pyramid.

We are calm, we are deliberate, we are confident because we are prepared.

We four strong young men form the foundation.

Above us are my sister and her husband.

My mom is on the third tier.

And then—the coup de grace—Vinicio Vazquez, Erendira's dad, sits upon my mother's shoulders.

The eight-person pyramid is executed perfectly. The response is tremendous. A world record is set. And, to make things even sweeter, at the end of the engagement the promoter pays us in full. After paying my troupe and expenses, I'm left with very little, but that's the least of it. As far as I'm concerned, it's mission accomplished.

I'm exuberant. Who wouldn't be? I've booked and pulled off a news-making event of my own. I figure that from here on out it'll be smooth sailing.

I figure wrong.

# 10

# One Night Only— Garth Brooks!

It's 8:00 a.m. and the union man has had his breakfast and is on his way to work. The Ford pickup is gassed up and ready to roll. It's an hour drive from Sarasota to Tampa. The Florida winter morning is clear and mild.

On I-275, he cranks up Creed's "With Arms Wide Open," one of his favorite rock anthems. The music energizes him and reaffirms his faith in a God that is good all the time. As he approaches the Sunshine Skyway Bridge, he marvels at the magnificent construction. His heart is singing.

In front of the big Tampa arena he looks at the neon sign that screams, "One Night Only—Garth Brooks!" He pulls into the employee parking lot, grabs his lunch box, and makes his way inside.

He punches the time clock and for the next six hours he, along with his fellow workers, does the manual labor of rigging the show. He hangs the chain motors. He works the fly rails that control the curtains. He does whatever's necessary to make sure the mechanical side of the show goes on without a hitch.

When the work is over, he doesn't stay for the show. Nothing against Garth Brooks—the man's a fine country singer—but it's time to be with the family. He punches out and heads home. He'll be back in a few days to help rig the show for David Copperfield. After that, it's Barry Manilow, Led Zeppelin, and Dolly Parton.

As a dues-paying member of the International Alliance of Theatrical Stage Employees, the man believes in honest labor. The man also makes no bones about the fact that he needs the money.

The man is me.

My father, already in the union, is the one who has facilitated my membership.

There's conflict between me and Dad. I see the glass half full and he sees it half empty. To my way of thinking he can be hardheaded and controlling. Yet his skills as a master carpenter and rigger have an enormous influence on me. I may not rise to his level in those areas, but I realize he still has much to teach me. Plus, his practicality keeps me on track when it comes to money.

I've seen that the road to financial freedom has lots of potholes. I was dead wrong that the Guinness record–setting eight-person pyramid would have the world clamoring for my next feat. For all the attention I got for that stunt, the world was strangely quiet in its aftermath. I'm reminded that the cold-blooded media have a frighteningly short attention span. What's hot news today is ancient history tomorrow. If a brand is to live, it must undergo continual reinvention. My world record is notable and gratifying, but, without improving upon it, it's getting me nowhere.

If the union isn't calling me, I'm calling John Carson at First Watch.

"I could use some work," I tell John.

"Well, Nik, I'd turn the job of general manager back over to you but I have a man in place."

"Who's doing the cooking?"

"We've got Mario and Ted in the mornings but Ted just quit. You interested in scrambling eggs?"

"No one's better at it than me."

"Tomorrow morning? Seven a.m.?"

"Look for me at six-thirty."

I scramble eggs, fry bacon, and chop up hash browns for the next few weeks. None of that stops me, though, from developing my sales approach as a performer. That means setting up a booth at the big convention of the International Association of Amusement Parks and Attractions that's attended by some forty thousand people.

To do the booth right—to advertise the feats of my Wallenda troupe—is a major investment. There are hundreds of other booths vying for attention: companies that construct rollercoasters, manufacturers of miniature golf courses and waterslides. Among seven miles of exhibits, my challenge is to make a splash in a ten-by-ten booth. I have the materials but lack the funds to pay for the space.

"How much do you need?" asks Joseph Mascitto, my closest friend in all the world.

I've known Joseph since we were kids together. He's a brilliant guy—an engineer—and the one person I can talk to about anything.

"Don't worry about it," I say. "I'll get the money."

"No you won't, Nik. You're all tapped out. You spent all your money on promotional materials. These booths aren't free. What are we talking about here?"

"Thousands."

"How many thousands?"

"Four."

"Fine. I've got your back."

"I don't want you to..."

"I know what you want, Nik. But more important, I know what you need. You need exposure. You need to make sure you have a presence at this convention. You need this booth."

Everyone needs a friend like Joseph. Over and again, he loans me money to keep me going—and then doesn't even care about being repaid. I'm careful to pay him back every dime, not because he'd ever ask for the money, but because my own sense of integrity is on the line.

On a spiritual level, Joseph is also a great confidant. There's no one I trust more to give me the deepest and wisest advice. In years to come he will help me see things to which I'm blinded.

What I can see, though, is that I have to work this massive convention and hustle up whatever engagements I can.

———

By 2002, we are a family of four—Erendira has given birth to our wonderful second son, Amadaos—and I'm overjoyed.

I also feel overwhelmed by a need to get back out there and put on a show. Erendira is just as eager to perform as I am. Meanwhile, the booth has paid off. I've booked an engagement at Coney Island in Cincinnati and for a three-month summer engagement. We're set to do sway poles and, the highlight of the act, a stunt that has me driving a motorcycle up an inclined cable.

The motorcycle breaks down.

It's a hand-me-down from Mom and Dad and beyond repair. This happens our first week in Ohio. No money to replace it—but no problem. Instead of riding the bike up the wire, I walk the three-hundred-foot cable. I'm also walking on air when I learn that Erendira is pregnant with our third child.

In 2003, the beautiful Evita enters the world and our family is complete.

My heart is filled with gratitude. I have the family of my dreams. My wife, two sons, and daughter are—and will always be—my heart.

The human heart, a magnificent creation of God, is a highly complex machine. It pumps blood and sustains life. But it also contains feelings of warmth and love, loyalty and trust.

I can feel that my heart is also connected to my drive. The thought of making my mark—in new and dramatic ways—continues to haunt me night and day.

"Sometimes," says my father, "a man can be too driven."

As a man in my young twenties, I don't like hearing that. I take his statement as a challenge.

"What do you mean?" I ask.

"You can't control everything and everyone around you."

"Is that what you think I'm doing?"

"I think that's what you're trying to do."

"Isn't that just called hard work?" I ask.

I'm not sure what my father is getting at. I'm just trying to nail down more high-visibility bookings. In doing so, if I'm relentless and run the risk of becoming a detail-obsessed control freak, I don't want to hear about it.

I want to hear that our engagement at the Wet 'n' Wild Emerald Pointed Water Park in North Carolina has come through. And it has!

"Can you handle it?" I ask Erendira, now a mother of three.

"Sure," she says without missing a beat.

"You ready to perform?"

"You don't have to ask me that, Nikolas. You know I am."

Erendira has been performing with her sisters and parents since she was a child. She and I were born into the world of pack-up-the-kids, hit the road, and entertain the people. Now we're packing up our kids and following the same road we've been following forever.

Or is it the same?

Yes and no.

Yes, Erendira and I are able to perform as a duo on the sway poles and revolving perch. Yes, during other engagements we join up with my parents and recruit others to execute a seven-person pyramid.

But no, I'm not happy doing the same-old same-old. I'm looking for the Next Big Thing. But until that happens, until I come up with a plan, we simply keep on keeping on.

In 2005, Erendira and I take our act to Raging Waters in San Dimas, California, while my parents and sister take over our spot at Wet 'n' Wild. The pattern of mixing and matching engagements and switching up family members is part of our collective strategy for survival.

When I'm back in Sarasota, I'm back on the call list of union men ready to rig the big shows at Van Wezel Performing Arts Hall. I continue to dream up schemes and stunts to bring us to the next level, but the dreams and schemes continue to elude me.

Then a break: McDonald's has a new premium roast coffee that they want to introduce through a high-wire act. They're willing to sponsor an entire show around a stunt. This comes at a moment when Erendira is superinvolved with the kids, so I turn to my sister, Lijana.

The McDonald's executive in charge wants to attract as much media as possible. He's come to the right guy. Do I have any ideas?

I do. "Imagine this," I say. "A wire is stretched between two cranes. My sister and I ride up on a hook attached to a rope. Now she's on top of her crane and I'm on top of mine. We walk out on the wire and meet in the middle."

"That doesn't sound all that exciting," says the exec.

"It will be," I say, "when we sit down in the middle of the cable and enjoy a cup of the new McDonald's coffee."

"You can do that?"

"I don't see why not. What do you say?"

"Go."

Just like that, I've planned my first skywalk—that is, a wire-crossing done outside an entertainment venue that is far higher and longer than your typical walk. This will be set up in downtown Detroit, where a street will shut down. The stunt will happen high above the Hard Rock Café.

At home in Sarasota, Lijana and I practice for a couple of weeks. My sister's the consummate professional but doesn't like the idea of sitting on the wire. She's more comfortable doing a split—her specialty—but after a series of rehearsals she's able to perfect the sitting move.

McDonald's does a great job with promotion. The film crews are out in force. Media are everywhere.

Lijana rides a rope hook up the crane to the wire—eighty feet high. On the other side I do the same. The wire is 125 feet long. We're each handed a cup of McDonald's coffee. In precise syncopation, we walk out on the wire and proceed until we meet in the middle. So far so good. When it's time to sit, though, I see that Lijana is nervous. So she does her split instead. Fine.

"Just stay calm," I tell her. "Gently move from your split to a sitting position."

She's muttering something under her breath—she doesn't like this stunt—but, following my lead, she's able to sit.

We raise our cups in the air in a salute to the hundreds of spectators below us, and then take a few sips. Having enjoyed the taste of a good java, I stand up, step over Lijana, and make my way to the top of her crane as she makes her way to mine.

I ride the rope down to street level. Lijana is set to do the same.

When I arrive at the bottom I look up to see that Lijana is still up there. Her crane has malfunctioned, creating a panic. The rope that will bring her down is not moving. It's stuck.

There's no way to get her down.

I look over at the men operating her crane and see fear in their eyes. They don't know what's wrong.

Don't ask me how, but I do. I have this strange instinct, this intuitive knowledge that feels like a gift from God. I realize that the boom is overloaded.

I signal to Lijana not to worry, but she is freaking out. She is convinced that she'll never get down safely. Her lips are saying, "I'm afraid, please help me, please do something *now*!"

"I have it all under control!" I shout. Of course I'm frightened inside but need to maintain outside composure. "Stay calm, Lijana! I'm coming to get you! It's all gonna be all right!"

Keeping my cool, I show the operator how to let off on the winch a little bit at a time. I tell the men operating the ropes to do the same. Then I jump on the rope and ride up on a hook. Lijana is still freaking out and I'm still urging her to stay calm. Finally I grab hold of her and lead her to the rope. She rides down and I follow.

We embrace, praising and thanking God for keeping our family safe. Our brother-sister bond is stronger than ever.

The press is all over the story—brother saves sister. The headline reads, "Hero of the High Wire." No one minds being called a hero, but I give credit to my dad. I'm the lucky inheritor of his great technical gift for mechanics. When it comes to the nuts and bolts of the business, I've been watching him since childhood. He's given me the knowledge that makes me feel that, no matter how complicated the stunt and the rigging that supports it, it's possible to be in control.

That's a great feeling, but also a dangerous one. If you feel like you can control something as precise as rigging, it's easy to fool yourself into believing that you control absolutely everything.

Control is a tricky commodity. Seems like the more I have, the more I want. I don't see that as a bad thing. I want to be in control of my craft. I want to be in control of my career.

But what about my wife?

How is she feeling about my controlling nature?

# 11

# The Joy of Dancing

You're my husband, not my father."

"Isn't that kind of obvious?"

"If it's so obvious, why are you acting like my father?"

"I'm not. I just get worried when you and the kids don't get back from the mall when you said you would."

"The shopping took a little bit longer."

"You should have called."

"You should have relaxed."

"I was afraid something had happened."

"What could have happened?"

"A car wreck."

"You're always imagining disasters, Nik."

"That only happens when I don't know where you are."

"That's not my problem," says Erendira.

"You could be a little more understanding," I say.

"You could be a little less commanding," she says.

"I believe that the man is the head of the household."

"I thought God was supposed to be the head of the household. Aren't you confusing yourself with God?"

When God is introduced into our argument, I pause. After our marriage, Erendira deepened her relationship with God. She became an impassioned follower of Jesus. In becoming a mother, she has deepened her capacity for love. She lavishes a sweet tenderness on our children that never fails to move me.

I also love them with all my heart. I like to think that I'm a strong emotional provider for my kids, but, given my extreme commitment to work, that role is primarily filled by Erendira. Her maternal care is a beautiful thing.

My own mother, also a devoted Christian, is a woman who, unlike Erendira, does not challenge her man. She accepts him as our family leader. In our home, Dad's word is law. That's the only kind of husband/wife relationship I've seen. Even though my mother earned her own reputation as a gifted performer, she has always acquiesced to Dad's plans. He was the director and we were his subordinates—that is, until I had my own family and became a director myself.

Isn't that the way it's supposed to work?

Not if you're married to a woman as fiery as Erendira.

Growing up, she witnessed her father's disloyalty to her mother. That did not help her develop trust in men. Unlike my mother and father, her parents were not disciplinarians. Erendira and her sisters were largely left to their own devices. So when she and I began a family on our own, I naturally stepped into the role of enforcer.

I believe this is a vital role. It comes naturally to me. Who can deny the fact that the psychological health of a family depends on firm guidelines and clear boundaries?

"Who can deny the fact that you treat me like a child?" says Erendira.

The accusation puzzles me. I love Erendira. I don't see her as child. I see her as a gorgeous woman, incredible artist, and loving mother.

"What are you talking about?" I hear myself asking her. "I treat you as my wife, not a child."

"You treat me like someone who needs close supervision. You treat me like someone who must fall into line."

"You make me sound like an army sergeant."

"Well…"

"You're exaggerating."

"You don't see yourself, Nik. You don't hear yourself."

Anything I say will sound defensive, so I leave the argument alone.

We return to our routine. I'm out there working union jobs at the arena, I'm setting up booths at the big amusement conventions, I'm doing all I can to keep the family business afloat.

Erendira is behind my effort to build the brand. When it comes to business, she's with me a hundred percent. She wants to perform as much as I do. Unlike my dad, who can't help but express some skepticism at my latest schemes, Erendira is always encouraging. She believes in me and

I believe in her. But that doesn't stop the growing tension between us.

—

It's Wednesday night. I'm just back from Tampa where I've done the rigging for Toby Keith.

"Mind taking care of the kids tonight?" asks Erendira.

I love spending time with my kids. "Not at all," I say, "but where are you going?"

"Dancing."

"Alone?"

"Of course not alone. I'm going out dancing with the girls."

Erendira loves dancing. She and her sisters have danced ever since they were little girls. Her family life was filled with music. Everyone played an instrument. I understand that dancing gives her joy. But...

"I'm not sure that's such a good idea," I say.

"I think it's a great idea."

"What club are you going to?"

"The one we always go to."

"I'm not sure it's safe."

"It's very safe."

"Some drunk could get out of control and..."

"Please, Nik, don't start inventing scenarios."

"I don't like it."

"You don't have to like it. You just have to take care of the children."

"What time will you be home?"

"Do I have a curfew?"

"That's not what I meant."

"That *is* what you meant. I'm not even answering the question."

"Look, Erendira, I don't feel good about this. I don't think you should go."

"You made yourself clear, Nik. But I'm going."

A half-hour later she's out the door.

I cherish my time with the kids. I love playing the part of a clown with them. I love seeing them laugh. I love telling them stories and putting them to bed. But for all the great pleasures of fatherhood, I can't stop worrying about Erendira. It isn't a question of jealousy or trust. I know she's the most faithful of wives. I know she simply wants to do what she loves doing—dancing. Dancing is healthy, dancing is creative, dancing is a wonderful way to expend energy. There's nothing in the world wrong with dancing. Except...

It's ten o'clock and Erendira is not home. I start worrying.

At eleven I worry even more. Erendira is right when she says I start imagining disasters. There was a fire in the dance club. There was a gas explosion. A car accident. A terrible collision.

She gets home at midnight, happy as she can be. I'm a wreck.

"Have fun?" I ask.

"Yes," she says. "It was fabulous."

"Okay," I say, "but this is the last time. I just can't allow this."

She doesn't bother to answer me. Her look of disdain says it all.

—

I try to back off, but I don't really understand that I'm being an authoritarian. I see myself as being reasonable. It's only reasonable that Erendira adhere to my sense of family order.

It's also only reasonable that, from time to time, we work in conjunction with my mom and dad. When I book an engagement that involves the seven-person pyramid I like hiring my parents. Not only is Mom a great aerialist, but Dad, although he no longer walks the wire, is a superb rigger.

The inclusion of extended family always makes the kids happy. They adore their grandparents and vice versa. But traveling and working with her in-laws does not always thrill Erendira. Mom is no problem. She has a sweet nature. But, for Erendira, Dad often exhibits the kind of authoritarian attitude that she finds objectionable in me.

"You're asking me to cut out my parents?" I say.

"No, they're part of our lives and I wouldn't want it any other way. I'm just saying on these long engagements I'd rather it'd be just us and the kids."

"Financially, my parents need my help."

"I'm not sure that's your responsibility."

"I'm not sure it isn't. They took care of me."

"They're strong people, Nik. They're talented people. They can take care of themselves."

"Well, you'll adjust. You'll be fine with it. It'll all work out."

"That's wishful thinking."

—

I wish that all the tension in our marriage would simply melt away. I wish that there could be nothing but harmony. I wish that Erendira could understand that there's nothing more important in my life than the happiness of my family—and that my tenacious work comes out of a deep need to make sure they are safe and secure.

She wishes that I could see her side of things. She wishes that I could understand what it means to have an equal partner, not a subservient one. She wishes that my need to grab the steering wheel and never let go could be tempered. She wishes that I could let her live her life on her own terms and in her own way.

James 4:10 says, "Humble yourselves in the sight of the Lord, and He will lift you up."

When I think of the Lord, when I pray to the Lord, when I address His mighty spirit, I have to be humble. I have to think that He is worthy while I am not. I am a broken vessel. It is only through His love that I am saved from an attitude that sees me—and not Him—as God.

And yet the more work I do to accomplish my goal, the more recognition I get, the more confident I become. Because it is through my tireless effort that I am making a name for myself, I see myself becoming arrogant. I don't like this and yet I know that sometimes a little swagger is necessary.

A new stunt no one has ever done before?

*I can invent one. I can do it. Leave that up to me.*

Massive press coverage.

*No problem. I always have a story the press will love.*

Flawless execution of the stunt itself.

Failure isn't an option. I'll keep going. I'll never stop. It's not in my blood to quit. My mantra is *Never give up!* I must manifest this mantra in everything I do.

My wife has to understand all this. My wife has to realize that she is married to no ordinary man. My wife has to see things my way.

Ephesians 5:22 says it: "Wives, submit to your own husbands as to the Lord."

And 1 Corinthians 11:3 says, "But I want you to know that the head of every man is Christ, the head of woman is man, and the head of Christ is God."

Erendira says: "I can't stand it when people use Scripture to win an argument. Scripture isn't a tool to win a debate. Scripture is about deepening your understanding and love of God—not beating down your opponent."

"I'm not your opponent," I say. "I'm your husband who loves you with all my heart."

We embrace, and the argument stops. There are many such moments of reconciliation and peace. But the issue doesn't go away. And neither does my passion for finding a way to break out, break through, and break another world record.

# 12
# Genius Clown for Jesus

Bello Nock is my hero, one of the greatest clown acrobat/ aerial artists of all time. My admiration and affection for him go back to when I met him as a kid. For years I wanted to be just like him. I even grew my hair and combed it in the sky-high crew-cut style that's Bello's trademark.

Ten years older than me, Bello has always been an artist I've tried to emulate. Like me, he comes from a multigeneration family of famous performers. The Nerveless Nocks are known the world over. Bello's parents and mine have been friends forever. The Nocks are also devout Christians.

From the time I was thirteen, they've driven from their home in Port Charlotte, an hour south of Sarasota, and spent Saturday nights with us so we can all attend church Sunday morning. The Wallenda/Nock postchurch barbecues are a hallowed tradition.

Bello is a blast—a high-energy, upbeat guy who loves to goof off and, at the same time, is a serious daredevil clown of the highest order. His wife, Jenny, is a strong follower of Jesus. Together they're a shining example of a committed Christian couple.

As a teenager, I babysat their little boy. Whenever Bello called me to help him in any way, I ran. I polished his truck. I helped him clear his property in Port Charlotte. We marched through his land with machetes, clearing brush. I was also deeply impressed by his business acumen. Unlike my folks, who were always struggling to hold their heads above water, Bello's family made good money. When his father retired, he bought each of his four sons a beefy state-of-the-art Mercedes truck filled with circus equipment.

Based on the Nock family history and his own innovative talent, he had established his own profitable brand. For years he was the star attraction and reason behind the success of New York's Big Apple Circus.

Bello was always reaching for the stars. Being in his presence, my motivation soared.

Now that I have a family of my own, I feel a bit more equal in Bello's presence. But I will always see him as a cool older brother. I view him as something of a sage.

—

In 2006, our families are together for one of those fun Sunday picnics. We've played games and chased the kids around the yard. We've stuffed ourselves on smoked barbecue, fat ears of corn, and homemade pecan pie. The kids have quieted down. The light of day is slipping away, the sky turning pinkish greyish black.

Bello and I recall the great time we had a year earlier when we hung out in Los Angeles and went to the Magic Castle, an exclusive private club and showcase for the world's greatest magicians. It's a privilege to have dinner there; to me it's hallowed ground. It was in this special setting that Bello began discussing his big plans. He never stopped dreaming of new and different stunts.

"One day soon, Nik," he said, "we should work together. A crazy wild stunt that the world's never seen before. Something totally radical."

"I like it," I said.

"Well, let's create something together. You're the guy with the scientific mind. And I'm the clown."

"Right—except what other clown has ever been called 'the greatest athlete ever to see foot in the World's Famous Arena'?"

"Who said that about me?"

"The *New York Daily News* said it when you performed at Madison Square Garden last year."

That was last year, an occasion when we couldn't stop talking shop. This year, though, is different. We're with our families, have enjoyed a satisfying home-cooked meal, and are communicating on a deeper level.

We're talking about God.

One of the pleasures of being in the company of Bello and his wife, Jenny, is our shared faith. Jenny is an especially strong Christian.

Tonight we start talking about God. I mention the good works I've been doing at church. Jenny listens patiently.

"Good works are great," she says, "and I'm proud of you, Nik. You have a heart for God. But it sounds like you're trying to win Him over."

"Well," I say, "I do want to be pleasing in His sight."

"You already are."

"Does that mean good works don't count?" I ask.

"Not at all. Good works reap their own rewards, but I don't think they have anything to do with salvation."

"The harder we work, the better off we are on every level," I say. "Financial, psychological, and spiritual."

"You make it sound like we have to earn God's love. But the truth is that God's love is a given. It's a gift. We can't earn what we already have. Do you see what I mean?"

I'm not entirely sure. That's when Jenny mentions a preacher she follows—Joseph Prince.

"Have you heard of him?" she asks.

I haven't. But this discussion has me curious. Jenny gives me samples of his writings in addition to DVDs of his preaching.

Pastor Prince is a youthful man with longish black hair who does not dress in the garb of a conventional preacher. He wears leather jackets and sport shirts and speaks plainly and forcefully. He's the founder and senior pastor at New Creation, a twenty-four-thousand-member megachurch in Singapore. His message could not be more direct: that grace is not one of the many gospel messages; grace is neither a gospel topic nor a gospel theme. Grace *is* the gospel.

He quotes John 1:17, which says, "For the law was given through Moses, but grace and truth came through Jesus."

He quotes Paul in Acts 20:24: " But none of these things

move me; nor do I count my life dear to myself, so that I may finish my race with joy, and the ministry which I received from the Lord Jesus, to testify to the gospel of the grace of God."

He quotes Paul again in Galatians 1:6–7: "I marvel that you are turning away so soon from Him who called you in the grace of Christ, to a different gospel, which is not another; but there are some who trouble you and want to pervert the gospel of Christ."

Prince sees the perversion of the gospel as anything that moves us away from understanding the heart of the matter. Grace is the heart of the matter. God gives grace freely. Grace is unmerited and undeserved favor. Grace is shockingly simple. To receive grace requires nothing—no feats of bravery, no acts of devotion, no works of charity. Grace is the very nature of a God, who sacrificed His son for the sake of our salvation. We are free, finally free, of striving to achieve His approval.

He loves us as we are; He loves us in our imperfection. He loves us when we realize remarkable feats and He loves us when we don't. By doing wondrous things, we can't get Him to love us any more. Or by falling into sin, we can't get Him to love us any less. His love is pure, eternal, and, if we embrace it, healing. We don't have to try to get Him to love us. We simply have to accept the fact that He does.

What a concept!

It's almost too easy. As a life-long striver, it's hard for me to change my thinking. As a life-long competitor, I live for achievement and victory. I live in a world where victory comes only as a result of hard work. Victory must be merited. Whatever I have achieved, I have earned. I've never lived life outside a meritocracy—the better you get, the higher your reward.

Is that how I've viewed God—as a mighty force who must be placated and pleased? Is that the Old Testament version of God that has added to my worldly motivation? Have I been trying to satisfy God the same way I've been trying to satisfy the agents who book me and the spectators who come to see me perform? Have I subconsciously mixed up my drive to succeed with my drive to win God's approval?

If that is the case, I'm astounded. And I'm also relieved. I'm astounded that for so long I've misunderstood the essential meaning of the gospel. And I'm relieved to know that nothing further has to be done. I can relax in the bosom of the Lord, knowing that He is both my comfort and my strength. The presence of that comfort and strength is not dependent on me. I am dependent on Him. And my faith affirms that His presence and healing love will never wane.

As a result, I can exhale. When it comes to God, I can breathe easy. He has done the spectacular. He has realized the sacrifice. No feat of mine will ever rival His.

Through my discussions with Jenny and Bello and the writings of Joseph Prince, I have a new and exciting understanding of God. In many ways I feel free. On the other hand, the world is still here—and the world still operates as a meritocracy. The circus world does not mirror God's grace. Unlike God's boundless grace, the circus world requires achievement through acts. That world still has a hold on me and, I suspect, always will.

Nik's great-grandfather Karl, performing a trick that's never been duplicated: a handstand on the heads of two people.

Martha Wallenda, Nik's great-grandmother; and Alberto Zoppe, Nik's grandfather.

Nik's father (bottom front) and mother (on top) rehearsing for the film *The Great Wallendas*.

Dave Klukow, Nik's father (Terry Troffer), and Nik (age one) setting up a wire for a performance in 1980.

Nik already on the wire at age two, learning from his mom, Delilah, with sister, Lijana, in the background. Circus Vargus tent is in the background.

Nik (age six) at Bensons Animal Park in Hudson, New Hampshire, playing with one of the bears.

Nik (age six) kissing his mother on the cheek before her performance in the Rockies at Circus Flora.

Nik's first walk on the wheel of death at age eight.

Nik at age six or seven in Sarasota, where he still practices to this day.

Nik at age twelve, performing as a clown with his dogs.

Performing in Middletown, Ohio, with his family, at age fifteen. *(Photo by Tom Rhein)*

Nik's first performance, at age thirteen, on a wire in front of an audience in Old Forge, New York, in a park called Enchanted Forest.

Nik (age seventeen) and Erendira (age fifteen) when they started dating. Her dad and Nik's mom were performing at a music festival in Milwaukee, Wisconsin.

Nik's troupe performing the seven-person pyramid in Sarasota, Florida, in 2010: (bottom left to right) Nik Wallenda, Paul Lopez, Mike Duff, Jonah Finkelstein; (middle) Tony Hernandez, Amos Meirmanov; (top) Lijana Wallenda.

A seven-person pyramid re-created in Detroit, Michigan (1998), for the first time in front of a live audience since it fell in 1962. Nik is on the bottom row, second from the right. His father is on the far right, his mother is on top.

Performing in Kurashiki, Japan: Nik Wallenda (left) and Mike Duff on the bottom, Delilah Wallenda on top.

A World Record eight-person, four-layer pyramid: (bottom left to right) Tim Carlson, Mike Duff, Jonathan Taylor, Nik Wallenda; (middle) sister Lijana Wallenda, Tony Hernandez; (middle top) mother Delilah; (top) father-in-law Vinicio Vazquez.

Nik and Erendira
on a motorcycle and
riding on a wire
during their first
year of traveling on
their own, in 2002.
*(Photo by Tom Rhein)*

(From left to right)
Nik, his son Yanni,
and Nik's father in
costume prior to a
show in Sarasota,
Florida.

Nik inspecting cable in Newark right before setting his first two World Records on the bicycle.

Walking out to make a phone call.

On the phone with *The Today Show*'s Matt Lauer in Newark, New Jersey, 135 feet above the street.

In Newark 2008, on a tightrope 235 feet across and 135 feet high: Nik breaks a world record for the highest and longest bike ride on a high wire.

Nik and his family on the roof of the Prudential Center after his record-breaking performance, which aired on *The Today Show*.

At Kings Island in Mason, Ohio, walking to the top of the Eiffel Tower replica, re-creating a walk made by his great grandfather. *(Photo by Tom Rhein)*

Walking at Kings Island in Mason, Ohio, in 2009. *(Photo by Tom Rhein)*

Nik breaking another World Record by hanging from his teeth for 30 seconds, 280 feet above the ground, in Branson, Missouri, in 2011. *(Photo by Tim Stowe)*

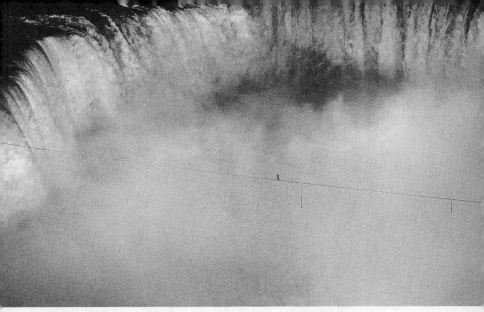

Nik's legendary walk across Niagara Falls in the summer of 2012.

Another view of the Niagara Falls walk, as seen from below. *(Photo by James P. McCoy)*

Photo was taken before Nik was honored as grand marshal of the Suncoast Offshore Parade in his hometown of Sarasota after his walk over the Grand Canyon. *(Photo by Tim Boyles Photography)*

God's grace is an incredible force of reassurance. But, no matter how deeply I embrace that gift, my view of the world is still rooted in striving and accomplishment. Ironically, my next major accomplishment will be forged alongside the man whose spiritual wisdom has brought me such solace.

Bello and I are about to do something entirely new, different, and daring.

# 13
# Wheeling and Dealing

It's the winter of 2006 and David Blaine is on the phone.

I've known and admired David for years. He's an amazing magician, illusionist, and world-record-setting endurance artist. He's also a master at getting press through TV specials and unprecedented stunts. David has forged a headline-making career with one spectacular stunt after another—burying himself in an underground plastic box for seven days, encasing himself in a block of ice for nearly sixty-four hours, standing atop a hundred-foot crane for thirty-five hours, living inside a transparent Plexiglas case suspended thirty feet over the River Thames for forty-four days.

"What's next?" I ask him.

"I'm calling it 'Drowned Alive,'" he says. "I'm submerging myself in a water-filled sphere eight feet deep. I'm putting it smack in the middle of the plaza at Lincoln Center here in New York City. I'll be in there for seven days and seven nights and I'd love for you to say hello. Would you mind dropping by?"

"I'd love to."

"That's great, Nik. The hecklers are always out in force, so seeing a friendly face always helps."

"Talking about friends, I think I'll invite Bello and his wife, Jenny, along."

"Bello is brilliant," says Blaine. "He's one of the real innovators. You and Bello are the guys who motivate me."

"Back at you, David. We'll be there."

Bello is up for the idea but suggests that Erendira and I first come to Albany, where he's featured at the Ringling Brothers Circus. From there we'll drive down to New York City and catch David at Lincoln Center.

Bello's act is astounding. Of all the circus performers in the world, no one approaches his gift for combining the whimsical humor of the clown with the daring grace of the aerialist. Like Blaine, he's a huge inspiration. He's all about creativity and courage.

After the show he introduces me to the boss.

"Nik Wallenda," he says, "this is Nicole Feld."

Ms. Feld runs the Ringling Brothers Circus, which has been owned by her family for over four decades.

"Pleasure to meet you," I say.

"My pleasure," says Ms. Feld. "I've long admired your family. They're part of Ringling Brothers history."

"It's been quite a while since a Wallenda performed at Ringling Brothers."

"I believe 1946 was the last time your great-grandfather Karl headlined the Greatest Show on Earth."

"You know your history well."

"No one will ever forget Karl Wallenda and the family he led with such flair and skill."

"Thank you, Ms. Feld."

"I'm hoping that the tradition will continue. I'd love to see another Wallenda rejoin our circus and continue the tradition."

"That would be wonderful," I say.

———

During the subsequent drive down to New York, Bello, Jenny, Erendira, and I talk about everything under the sun. We have a world in common: an abiding belief in Christ and a passion for dreaming up spectacular stunts.

Because we're on our way to see Blaine, one of the young princes of the spectacular stunt, stunts are on our minds—how to make them bigger, better, and even more audacious.

We check into a midtown hotel and go for dinner at the Olive Garden in Times Square. Endless breadsticks. Endless shop talk.

Here comes the pasta and the veal, the calamari and the chicken cacciatore. As we start eating, our shop talk intensifies. In between bites of scampi, Bello grabs a napkin and starts drawing.

"What do you think?" he asks, showing me his sketch.

"Looks like the Wheel of Death," I say, referring to the huge revolving structure, usually thirty-nine feet tall, that looks like two giant hamster wheels connected by an axle.

"It is," he says. "But the world has already seen this."

"Many times. People still love it."

"I know, but I think people live for surprise. They want to see something different. So let's give them something different. Instead of two wheels, let's double it. Let's give them four."

"That would be amazing. How would it work?"

"You would start out in one wheel..."

"Me?" I ask. "You want me to do this with you?"

"That's the whole point," says Bello. "We've been wanting to work together for years. Well, this is the perfect opportunity. You start out in one wheel, I'm in the other, we do our usual tricks and then—boom!—fireworks go off and suddenly the wheels split apart and there are four!"

"Incredible!"

"I think so."

"Who's going to design all this?"

"You are," says Bello. "You're Mr. Mechanics."

"I'd need help."

"You have help. You have your father and his brothers. You have a whole family of genius engineers behind you."

"It wouldn't be easy."

"Nothing this innovative is ever easy."

"I'm sure we could do it," I say.

"Now you're talking. How long would it take you to figure it out?"

"No more than a few months," I say with my usual optimism.

"Might be more than a few."

"And you'd try to sell to Ringling Brothers?" I ask.

"I'm pretty sure Ringling would go for it. How do you feel about working for them?"

"John Ringling was the reason my great-grandfather left Europe. Ringling invited him to America in 1928. Ringling sounds right."

"Done right, I think this concept of a quadruple wheel can make headlines."

"Shouldn't there be a story attached to the act?" asks Erendira.

"What kind of story?" I wonder.

"Bello is in one of the wheels and you, Nik, are in the other, right?"

"Right."

"Well, what if the two of you are fighting over a girl? To gain her attention and prove your valor, you two make all sorts of moves—back flips, somersaults, rope tricks. Who will win over her heart?"

"And you, Erendira, could play the part," says Bello.

"Perfect," I say. "It'll be sensational."

For the rest of the dinner we plot and plan. One Wheel of Death becoming two becoming four is the most exciting idea I've heard in years. And that the stunt will include Erendira makes it that much better.

I'm over the moon.

David Blaine is underwater.

He's sitting in this sphere of water. He's wearing handcuffs and his feet are chained. An enormous crowd surrounds him in the plaza at Lincoln Center. Some are cheering, some are jeering, but overall the mood is upbeat. He's been "drowning alive" for five days and five nights with two more to go. Bello, Jenny, Erendira, and I stand in front of the sphere, look David in the eye, and give him a big thumbs-up. He breaks into a big smile. We hang out for a while, letting him know that he has our full support and admiration. He seems pleased.

"He seems a little crazy," says Erendira.

"Not crazier than me," I say.

My wife doesn't disagree.

"Guys like David keep us going," says Bello. "They reaffirm the fact that the impossible isn't impossible at all."

A few minutes later I'm introduced to Shelley Ross, a woman who serves as the executive producer of Blaine's television special.

"I know who you are, Nik Wallenda," she says. "You're a supertalented guy and I think you need a television special of your own."

Naturally, her words are music to my ears.

"I would love it," I say. "But how do I make it happen?"

"You might start by talking to my husband, David Simone. He's a manager."

I call David. We have a great talk but don't yet forge a plan. A couple of things have to happen first.

—

"Do you think it's possible that this new scheme of yours won't work?" asks my dad when I get back from New York. "The mechanics may be unworkable or, at the very least, undependable. Are you really sure that you and Bello can stand balanced on top of twin circles thirty-nine feet in the air?"

"I am sure."

So is Bello. We get to work in his backyard workshop. The idea we pursue is this: When we first come out on the wheels we want the audience to think they're connected. Then a blast of fireworks and suddenly the wheels split and go off in opposite directions.

Much of the drama comes from the self-perpetuating nature of our stance on the wheels. There are no motors or engines. Our footwork and footwork alone will set the wheels in motion. To remain vertical, we have to run in place at twenty miles an hour. And before the wheels split off, we must run in perfect synchronicity. If I run faster or slower than Bello, the wheel loses its balance. There are no safety nets beneath and we choose not to wear harnesses. Harnesses and nets are distractions.

It's a tricky business, especially since the wheels have to be custom-constructed. The first problem is that the axle, around which the wheels rotate, continues to bend. Ultimately this means the axle will break. If this happens during the act itself, the result will be fatal. If we can't find a nonbendable axle, my father will be right. All in vain.

"I'm afraid this whole thing, while a magnificent and bold idea, just may not be doable," says Dad.

I turn to Dad's brother-in-law, Timothy Stephenson, an engineer and the chief metallurgist for the National Aeronautics and Space Administration. I explain the problem to him. Intrigued by the challenge, Uncle Tim goes right to work. In his lab, he begins to experiment with hardened steel alloys.

"Is that going to work?" I ask.

"It's worth testing," he says.

After a couple of weeks of intense experimentation, Uncle Tim has custom-blended several hard steel alloys and finally found the one mix that he's certain will not bend or break.

I tell Bello that we have the axle we need.

Bello tells Ringling Brothers, which is underwriting our efforts and will feature the stunt in its Greatest Show on Earth, that we're ready to go into production. They want to know the cost. We put paper to pencil and come up with a big number—well over one hundred thousand dollars.

Bello lets them know. Worried that the high price tag might blow the project out of the water, we hold our breath.

A few days later, Bello calls.

"Production costs approved," he says, "but something else has not been approved."

"What's that?"

"They don't want to call it the Wheel of Death."

"Why not?"

"They think it's too negative, too scary."

"Circuses have been calling it the Wheel of Death for decades. Fans know it by that name. It's a great name. It implies danger and daring."

"Ringling doesn't want to imply death," says Bello. "Remember Neville Campbell, the Englishman who performed on the wheel in 1994?"

"I do. He was a young guy, only twenty. He lost control during the act and fell some fifteen feet..."

"And died. Ringling doesn't want to conjure up memories of death."

"So what do they want to call it? The Wheel of Life?"

"The Wheel of Steel."

"The Wheel of Steel is cool," I say, "as long as we still have a deal."

"We do," says Bello. "They also want to name the entire show after me."

"Wow! Has Ringling ever done that before?"

"Never in their history. They want to call it Bellobration. What do you think?"

"I think you deserve it, and I'm happy to be along for the ride."

"I just want to keep testing out that metal and make sure it does what your uncle says it will."

The metal passes the test, holds firm, and, doing our hijinks inside the wheel, we're feeling steadier with every passing day.

With a new name for the stunt and a new name for the entire show, Bello and I are ready to roll. After months of arduous practice in his backyard, here comes Bellobration.

—

Bellobration debuts in Tampa. The press has been primed and pumped. The public has expressed curiosity. Ringling has gone all out. There are Bellobration ads and posters everywhere you look.

The opening is spectacular. There's an original song celebrating Bellobration. There are elephants and dozens of Bellolike clowns who, with their sky-high flaming-red crew cuts, are dressed to mirror the man himself.

The man himself is introduced with great fanfare. It's

Bello—Mr. Exuberance, Mr. Upbeat, Mr. Fun, a fabulous character who combines the floppy charm of a clown with the sleek audacity of a daredevil. Everyone, from grandparents to grandkids, loves Bello.

Bello and Erendira perform on two sway poles, some seventy-three feet tall. The poles sway twenty feet in every direction. They expand the repertoire, doing more elaborate tricks as they leap from one pole to the other. All this happens in the first half of the show.

In the second half, after a variety of other circus acts, it's time for the main attraction, the Wheel of Steel. Even in its traditional guise—a double wheel revolving thirty-nine feet off the ground—the act is nothing less than spectacular. The crowd is amazed at our dexterity inside our individual wheels. We run, jump, flip, and twist ourselves in every position imaginable. But then comes the moment: The lights go dim and, after a thunderous boom, fireworks explode and suddenly the double wheel duplicates itself and there are four spinning cylinders. The crowd gasps. The crowd loves it. The press loves it. The reviews are off the chart. The crowds grow. In its first-time-ever package named for a single performer, the Greatest Show on Earth has refurbished its image. We tour for over two years, playing before 5 million people in eighty cities. Any way you look at it, Bellobration is a hit show.

# 14

# Raw Ego

It's 2007 and I'm twenty-eight years old. We're on a brief break from Bellobration. I'm back home in Sarasota. It's early morning. Erendira and the kids are still asleep.

I'm up early. I make a pot of coffee, a couple pieces of toast, and sit down for my morning devotion. Every morning is a good morning to talk to God.

I open the Bible to John. I love John's unbridled enthusiasm and great love for the Lord. John never fails to move me. I especially cherish John 3:16, one of my favorite of all passages, which says, "For God so loved the world that He gave His only begotten Son, that whoever believes in Him shall not perish but have eternal life." My eyes go down the page to John 3:21: "But he who does the truth comes to the Light, so that his deeds may be clearly seen, that they have been done in God."

I want to live in the light. I want my deeds to reflect that light. I want to be seen as a man whose accomplishments are the result of faith. I want the glory to go to God.

But I also want to amplify those accomplishments. And, if I am to be honest, I want a degree of glory for myself. My love of the Lord and my raw ego exist together.

"Your ego comes on like he's your best friend," says a Christian elder whose spiritual wisdom I seek, "but he also wants to kill you."

"I'm not sure what that means."

"Your ego seeks praise. Your ego seeks the world's attention and the world's validation. Your ego gives you the idea that he's protecting you from starvation or neglect. But your ego can't get enough attention. He can't get enough praise. Your ego needs to grab all the glory. Your ego will sap your spirit with its insatiable need for adulation. Your raw ego sees itself, and not God, as the center of your world."

"But no one can cut himself off from his ego," I say. "Isn't it your ego that gives you the motivation to get out there and do the impossible?"

"Your ego is part of you," says the elder. "And yes, your ego is part of your motivation—to be seen, recognized, and appreciated."

"I grew up in a world of big-time egos," I say. "You can't be a circus performer and not have a big ego. It goes with the territory. My forebears all had giant-sized egos. Each of them yearned for greater fame and immortality."

"In your business egomania may be an occupational hazard."

"It is," I say.

"That won't change. But what can change is your conscious

recognition of your ego. If the ego's compulsive appetite is recognized, we have a chance to curb it. We need to step out of our ego and look back at it. We need distance from our ego. Yes, it's powerful; yes, it's always going to be there. But does it have to control us?"

"I keep hearing that word 'control,'" I say. "My wife is convinced I want to control her and every last detail of her life."

"Do you?"

"I don't think so. I just don't like the feeling of being out of control. I've always thought being in control is a good thing."

"It is—in certain areas. In others, it's not. I guess the paradox is feeling that we must be in control while, at the same time, knowing that it's God who's in control."

"And does that mean," I ask, "giving up all control?"

"No. It means being thoughtful and reflective about when your raw ego, and not God, is ruling your spirit."

—

Conversations like this are helpful. I'm always in close touch with my spiritual mentors. Guys like Chris Ripo and Joseph Mascitto help me manage the thoughts running through my mind. But managing my ego is another challenge altogether.

As a part of Bellobration, I see the wondrous benefits of a show that features a single artist. I'm glad to contribute to Bello's celebrity. With my red-haired crew cut piled high like his, I'm happy to be a Bello disciple. He's a generous mentor of mine, plus he's an incredible artist. But I also can't see myself continuing to work in his shadow. I have too high an opinion of my own skills not to pursue greater stardom for myself.

Is that ego?

Yes.

But is that attitude necessary to get where I want to go?

Yes.

Bello is the first guy to encourage me to step out on my own again, and in his encouragement I detect a note of hesitancy. We are two highly competitive men. Were we not, we couldn't be leaders in our field. We both see ourselves as champions. I have certainly championed his cause and I feel that he wants to champion mine. But that is difficult for him. I certainly understand. Were I the ruling king I might also be hesitant about encouraging a young upstart. Being brothers in Christ doesn't mean that our raw egos are not overactive. We are two overdriven men.

Friendship among men—especially ambitious men competing in the same field—is tricky business. Even when such friendships are based on mutual respect, they aren't easy to maintain. I try. And I believe Bello tries, but I also know that both of us realize that I have to go my own way. I suspect that the thought—that I might come up with the next big thing—might make Bello a little uneasy.

No matter, as Bellobration winds down, I realize I need to wind up the Nik Wallenda brand. This is when my conversations with David Simone become more frequent. He and partner Winston Simone—they share a last name but are not related—run a top-flight management firm. They're seasoned professionals with great contacts in the entertainment world of big-time media. They sense my ambition, I sense theirs, and I'm eager to work with them.

"We like you, Nik," says Winston. "You've got a good personality. You've got the All-American look, and you do all these mind-bending feats. But before we sign you up, we need something tangible to show a promoter. Give us a call when you have an idea for a big project—something, for instance, that can turn into a TV special."

I love the idea of a TV special, but, in truth, I don't have an idea. I tell Winston and David that I'll be in touch as soon as I do.

My mind starts reeling. I need to come up with something big. Meanwhile, family first. I have a short winter vacation planned in Orlando.

I'm happy to go, happy to take a short break from Ringling, happy to be with Erendira and the kids. We do Disney World, exploring everything from Epcot to Magic Kingdom Park to Typhoon Lagoon. The kids have a blast. Erendira is relaxed, but I'm not. My mind can't stop searching for the idea that could enlist the Simones as my managers.

"It needs to be something never done before," I tell Erendira.

"That's what you always say, Nik. And you always manage to come up with something."

"But this can't be just another pyramid or a trick on the wire."

"I understand," says Erendira. "It has to be grand enough to merit its own TV special."

"What did you just say?"

"You heard me, Nik. I said it has to be grand enough to merit a television special."

"Grand. You used the word 'grand.' Something grand. Well, isn't the Grand Canyon grand?"

"You mean walk across the Grand Canyon?"

"Why not?"

"At what point?"

"There's probably any number of feasible points. I'm sure that could be figured out. But can you imagine it, Erendira, can you envision the drama of such a walk?"

"I can. I think it's the idea you've been looking for."

"That's the kind of idea we can sell," says Winston Simone when I call him the next day. "Let me see if I can set the wheels in motion."

The wheels start spinning. I'm walking around Disney World's Blizzard Beach with the family when my cell rings. It's David Simone.

"Can you be in New York tomorrow?" he asks.

"What for?"

"The William Morris Agency thinks they can package your Grand Canyon walk. They want to meet you."

"I'm there."

"You're cutting short our vacation?" asks Erendira when I tell her what's happening.

"I have to, honey. This is major."

"I understand."

"You stay. There's no reason for you and the kids to leave."

They stay. I go.

I'm sitting in the office of a senior William Morris agent. David and Winston Simone are seated beside me. The agent wants to hear my vision. I paint the picture. He buys it.

I and my ego are riding high.

A couple of weeks later I'm flying to L.A. to meet with executives from ABC, NBC, CBS, and Fox. I keep painting the picture, and everyone keeps buying it. Everyone loves the idea. NBC loves it most.

NBC flies me to New York for more meetings with more top-ranking execs. The final meeting is in the executive dining room on the top floor of Rockefeller Center. All the world is at our feet. A private chef prepares our lunch. The execs want to hear my vision of this walk one final time.

I articulate the vision for them. They're sold.

We're set. Lawyers get involved. Lawyers have no trouble working it out. Permits are obtained. Engineering plans are set into motion.

I call my uncle Mike, who's in Baghdad locating and disabling land mines. My dad is often on edge, while Uncle Mike never loses his cool. From his bunker, he's whispering information to me and my dad on how to rig the wire across the cable.

"Is it a done deal?" he asks.

"Not completely," says my dad.

"What do you mean?" I say. "NBC has already bought the cable."

"Final contracts haven't been signed," Dad points out.

"They will be."

"Either way," says Uncle Mike, "I'll be sending more specs in a couple of days."

I'm thrilled.

"It's my first television special," I tell Bello, with whom I'm still performing at Ringling.

"TV specials are nearly impossible to pull off," he says.

"Well, I've pulled this one off," I assure him.

I call all my friends—Chris Ripo, Mike Duff, Joseph Mascitto.

Dad remains skeptical, but that's Dad. I don't even bother to argue. This has to happen. My ego is on the line. Too many elements have unexpectedly come together for it to fall apart. We have only a couple of minor points left in the final negotiations. Contracts will be signed in a matter of days. It's a lock.

And then the lock breaks.

The call comes from Winston Simone.

"There's turmoil at NBC," he says. "Our guy—the man in charge of specials—is out."

"What does that mean for us?" I ask.

"Our main supporter has been fired."

"Who's the new man?"

"I'm not sure, but from what I hear he's coming with a hatchet. The network is looking to cut budgets."

"But they've already bought the cable. That's a major investment. They wouldn't turn back now, would they?"

"It isn't a matter of 'they,'" says Winston. "It's a matter of 'he'—whoever he turns out to be."

He turns out to be a cost-cutting crusader. The new man in charge of specials sees nothing special about my walk. All he sees is red ink. And just like that, the project is scrubbed.

I feel like a fool. My ego deflates like a balloon.

I counted my chickens before they were hatched. I went and bragged to everyone I knew.

It's tough telling Bello what happened.

"How's the special going?" he asks after one of the shows on the Wheel of Steel.

"It's not," I say.

"What happened?"

"Change of regime at NBC. New guy says it's too expensive."

"That's rough," says Bello.

Dad says the same thing.

Mike Duff says, "You'll get 'em next time."

I need the encouragement because I'm feeling like an idiot. The idea of my own TV special had me ego-tripping like no one's business.

Had I been cruising for a bruising? Did the fact that I had boasted about my great accomplishment before realizing that accomplishment indicate that I was more pompous than I was practical?

The answer is yes. The answer is that boastfulness may be as much a part of my nature as gutsiness. The answer is that there are still lessons I need to learn. And although those lessons—those endless lessons—are about humility, I'm still up late at night trying to figure out the next big idea.

———

The idea comes out of that one ingredient so essential to successful show business—promotion. Ringling wants to promote the final Bellobration show at Newark's Prudential Center. Newark wants to promote this new eighteen-thousand-seat arena. And of course I'm looking to promote myself. I'm looking to enter the big-boy arena where I can stand beside artists like Bello and Blaine.

I swing into action. I propose a skywalk between the Prudential Center—135 feet high—and a crane. I'll walk from the roof of the Center to the top of the crane. But that's when everything will change. At the crane, I'll be handed a bike, mount it, and ride back across. That bike ride, 235 feet long, will be the longest high-wire bike ride in history. Not only will I do this, but I'll do it live on NBC's *Today* show before a nationwide audience of millions. The hookup with NBC comes about through the extraordinary intervention of Shelley Ross, whose influence with the network producers is the main reason I get this amazing coverage.

"Are you sure you can pull this off?" asks my dad. "Are you certain it's plausible?"

"Perfectly plausible," I answer. "It's just a matter of getting our ducks in a row."

The ducks line up.

Ringling is willing.

The Prudential Center says yes.

The *Today* show is on board.

I sense that deep down Bello may not be all that crazy about the idea, but he says yes. Bello's going to support me.

—

October 15, 2008. Erendira, Yanni, Amadaos, and Evita are by my side, atop the Prudential Center. I give each of them a big hug and kiss. My dad is on the ground below. He's been working for days to make sure that the rigging is right.

Now the NBC cameras are trained on me. Matt Lauer, Ann Curry, and Meredith Vieira are in the New York studio doing the commentary. They describe my every move.

Cloudless sky. Ten miles in the distance I can see the skyscrapers of Manhattan. The Empire State and Chrysler buildings reflect the morning sun. The highways and bridges are crowded with commuters.

"Ready?" asks the producer.

"Ready," I say.

I step out on the wire, my forty-five-pound balancing pole firmly in hand. Clear sky, clear mind. Distant memories of being a boy and walking the wire when Mom and Dad would throw pine cones over my head to show me how to focus in the face of distractions. No distractions now. Just calm easy toe-to-heel walking. One step, then another, and then another.

When I reach the midway point, I sit down, pull a cell phone out of my pocket, and call the studio, just to check in with Matt, Ann, and Meredith. We chat for a while before I get back up and complete the walk. Just before I arrive, I experience a small slip. That happens. Nothing to worry about. I calmly reclaim my composure and make it to the top of the crane, where Bello is waiting to hand me my bike.

Now for the real show, the stunt designed to set a new world record.

The bike is not custom-made. I bought it off the rack and then removed the tires and the handlebars. The idea is to ride the tireless wheels over the cable. The wheels are neither concave nor custom-made. Just two plain tireless bike wheels.

I get on the bike. Bello hands me the balancing pole. And slowly I start to pedal. The ride is slow and steady. Naturally there is no net. There is never a net. There is the safety of a balance born of experience, a balance that is as natural as speaking or breathing, a balance that assures me the ride will go well. It proceeds apace. I am in the moment. I am feeling fine on this beautiful October morning. I am aware of the sounds of trains below and a helicopter above. I am aware of the flight of birds. I feel the warmth of the sun. I keep pedaling.

Only toward the very end, where the cable is inclined upward, does the bike seem to lock up. The bike starts to slip. I feel myself moving backward.

Dad and I are connected by headset, and I hear him exclaiming, "Don't back up!"

"I have to," I say.

"You can't. You're locked up. Whatever you do, don't back up!"

A thought flashes through my mind: *Am I going to fall?* I've never had this thought before. I've never come close to falling before. But this is different. This is a crisis of the first order.

"I'm telling you not to back up," Dad keeps repeating.

"I'm telling you that I have to."

For a few seconds I allow the bike to go backward before gently pressing the pedals forward. Little by little I apply slight pressure, just enough to turn the wheels. I feel myself moving forward. I'm back on track and gain enough momentum to reach the final destination, where my wife and children are waiting. Beautiful warm embraces.

A representative from the Guinness World Records is there. I'm given my certificate. Matt, Ann, and Meredith congratulate me.

The *Today* producers tell me that never before in the history of the show have they devoted a half-hour of live coverage to a single event. If my ego was excited before, it's now going crazy.

But it's more than ego.

"You seized the moment," says my friend Chris Ripo. "That's exactly what you were born to do."

"You're a born promoter," says Joseph Mascitto. "Plus you have the creativity to dream up promotion-worthy events."

"I'm proud of you," says Mike Duff. "I remember all those crazy dreams you talked about when we were kids. Well, now you're making those dreams come true."

Even my dad, skeptic of skeptics, had to say, "The event came off well, son. I don't see how this can hurt your career."

Hurt?

How about *make* my career?

That kind of exposure on the *Today* show put me in a new position. I suddenly had a national profile. Not to capitalize on this moment in time would be not only foolish, but fiscally irresponsible.

It's time to step up my game. My twenty-four months on Bellobration were great—but as a stepping-stone, not an end in itself. I have no interest in returning to Ringling. Even though it's a world record, my Prudential bike ride is hardly enough to convince the Greatest Show on Earth to create Wallendabration.

I need to come up with a greatest show of my own.

———

Not one show, I decide, but a series of shows. And not simply shows but a story that links them all together.

What is it that I do up there on the high wire?

I walk.

And wouldn't it be appealing—wouldn't it make for a great promotional story—if I decided to walk across America.

"What would that entail?" my father asks. "What kind of resources? What kind of money are we talking about?"

"I'm not sure. I was thinking of approaching Cedar Fair Amusement Parks."

"How would that work?"

"Well, they own over a dozen parks—from Knott's Berry Farm in California to Carowinds in North Carolina. You're talking about tens of millions of visitors a year."

"What makes you think they'll make the kind of major investment in you that's required?"

"I have no reason to think they won't, Dad. The *Today* show exposure has been tremendous. Plus I'm going to make a presentation to Cedar Fair that will spell out the publicity I can bring them. I don't see how they can turn it down."

"Big corporations can turn down anything they want to," says Dad. "You need them a lot more than they need you."

"Granted," I say, "but I'm still determined to make it work."

It does work. Turns out to be another step up. But in taking that step, I nearly stumble and crash—not in terms of the wire, but, more important, in my relationship with my wife.

I still don't understand how my marriage is on the line.

# 15

# The End of the Line

Your great-grandfather walked a wire from the front gate of the park to the halfway point of the replica of the Eiffel Tower," says a representative of King's Island, the Cedar Fair Amusement Park in Mason, Ohio, twenty-five miles northeast of Cincinnati.

"Wonder why he didn't walk the entire distance?"

"From what I understand, the rigging wasn't right. His people couldn't figure out a way to make it completely safe. It's a heck of a haul—262 feet high and 800 feet across. Have you ever done a walk that long, Nik?"

"No," I say. "But that's all the more reason to try. My dad's here as my chief rigger. I'm going to see if he thinks it's possible to run a cable all the way to the top."

"Well, that's one way to outdo the great Karl Wallenda."

I bristle at that remark. "I never want to outdo Karl, and

I never will. If I do this walk, it's my way of continuing what he started. In respect to my great-grandfather, it's always a matter of continuity. It's never competition. Given the technology available to him, the man did everything possible—and then some."

My dad surveys the scene and decides that yes, it's possible. Alert the press. Print up the posters. The walk is on.

The walk is the longest of my career—eight hundred feet, taking twenty-five minutes from entryway to the top of the tower.

The Walk Across America has me flying high. From city to city, the crowds grow in number. The drama is great. I love the larger crowds, I love the drama. As the headliner at Three Rivers Regatta, on the Fourth of July I'm set to walk two hundred feet above the Allegheny River in Pittsburgh, but there are problems.

"We specifically said that we require cable with absolutely no oil," says Mike Duff, who's been helping my dad do the rigging, "but this cable is greasy. It's covered in oil."

"Best to cancel," says Dad.

"Plus it's raining and they expect even stronger winds," says Mike.

"Just adds to the drama," I say.

"What about the oil?" asks Mike.

"Just bring my wire shoes," I say.

"Everyone will understand if you pull out," says my father.

"They will—but I won't. And I'm not."

When it comes time for the walk, I work to center myself, to remain settled and enter the zone of complete concentration. When I get to the top of the crane, Mike is there.

"You have my wire shoes?" I ask.

Mike goes white. "I can't believe it, Nik. I forgot them."

I pause a second before I say, "No problem. Probably better if I go in my socks. Better traction."

I take Mike's forgetfulness as a positive sign. After all, I'm wearing the kind of woven socks that will get me maximum traction. By the time I reach the top of the crane and step on the wire, the winds are howling. I look across—from end to end it's 1,084 feet, an even longer walk than King's Island.

I step out. A few minutes into the walk, I pause to kneel and wave to the huge crowd below. After all, they've come out to see me in the rain. The least I can do is acknowledge their presence. I get up and start moving across. A few seconds later, though, the winds pick up, and, at that moment, I decide to stop my forward motion for a few seconds. I do this not to excite the crowd but simply to insure my balance. I'm neither nervous nor unsteady, but merely cautious. My training has taught me that pausing can be useful. I've learned never to fight the elements, but rather to bend with them. Accept them. Embrace them. Allow them to lead you and feed your spirit with quiet strength.

My long pause has me even more centered. When I start up and begin to step, my socks are soaked from the rain. Rather than irritate me, the wetness feels good on my feet. I understand how wetness, rather than distract me from my goal, may well give me more traction. I accept the wetness not as a hindrance, but a gift.

All negatives can be turned positive.

I keep on walking, slowly, deliberately until, nearly a half-hour later, I reach the platform on the other side. I've crossed the Allegheny River in the rain and couldn't be happier. Below me, the crowd goes wild. I wave, thank the good people of Pittsburgh for this opportunity, and thank God for my life.

What could be better than this?

Because this is a series of skywalks, there's no need for other acts. That means at the end of the tour I can go home with more money that I can apply toward my next feat. But unfortunately that also means that Erendira, who is accompanying me, doesn't have the pleasure of performing.

Because I need to do preshow promotions, sometimes I fly from city to city while Erendira drives with my father in the truck hauling the rigging equipment. This doesn't make her happy. I know she'd rather be with me, but she's a trouper. She understands that we're on a tight budget. Besides, as a young girl, she traveled in conditions far worse than these. She's used to the rigors of the road.

She's with me at Cedar Point, the company's flagship park, in Sandusky, Ohio, where I'm scheduled to do a radio interview at a local station. I know Erendira isn't thrilled about having been on the road for nearly twelve weeks now. And I know being with her father-in-law can be a strain. At the same time, my mind is focused on the upcoming skywalk and my need to promote it.

We arrive at the radio station. I get out of the car but Erendira does not.

"Aren't you coming in?" I ask.

"You go on. I'll listen to it on the radio."

I enter the studio. It's a man/woman team doing the interview. They're extremely pleasant. The woman is attractive. They want to know all about my past achievements. They express great enthusiasm about my upcoming sky-walk. The conversation is fast-paced and pithy.

"One last question, Nik," asks the woman. "How long is your balancing pole?"

"That's kind of a personal question," I say. "Maybe you should ask me that when we're off the air."

Point well made. Everyone laughs. I'm pleased at myself for displaying some wit. When the interview is over, I go back out to the car.

Erendira is furious.

"What's wrong?" I ask.

"If you don't know, that makes it even worse."

"Know what?"

"What you said to that woman."

"About the balancing pole?"

"Oh, so you do know."

"It was a joke."

"It wasn't funny. It was crude and inappropriate."

"And you're jealous about a woman who I'll never see again?"

"It has nothing to do with jealousy. I'm fed up with your thoughtlessness. Your entire world is centered on you."

"You're reading that remark the wrong way," I say.

"You're telling me how to read remarks. You're telling me how to think. You want to control everyone and everything around you."

"You're just feeling..." I begin to say.

"I'm tired of the *you* messages. Tired of hearing you telling me how *I* feel."

"Well, I know that..."

"You think you know everything, Nik. You're like your father. You're a know-it-all. Well, just know this. I'm going home."

When we get back to the hotel, Erendira throws her clothes into a suitcase, climbs into the car and, without me, drives thirteen hundred miles to our home in Sarasota.

For the rest of my Walk Across America, I don't hear another word from her.

For the rest of my Walk Across America, I'm feeling numb. I know my wife is spirited. I know she is a force to be reckoned with. I know she can fly off the handle in ways that seem extreme. But this is a new development. She really did pack up her things and leave. She really is gone. And alone, I am left to try to understand what has happened.

I see myself as a strong man. I see myself as a proud man. I see myself as a man who spiritually cannot be separated from my family. I'm devastated.

For all the tensions in the family in which I was raised, it never fell apart. Mom stuck with Dad. Dad stuck with Mom. Mom and Dad stuck by their kids. And their kids stuck by them.

My relationship with my dad has never been easy, but my dad has always been part of my team. It's family first. It's one big family. But is it?

When I married Erendira, we moved in with Mom and Dad. We probably lived with them too long, but money was an issue. Our earnings were slim. And because I believe in savings, I had to find a way to preserve our meager income. I knew Erendira was not happy living under the same roof as my parents, but I was the man in charge. I was the one who kept saying that it isn't as bad as all that. After all, it's family.

———

"How would you feel if I forced you to move in with *my* family?" Erendira would ask me.

Because that wasn't a real possibility, I ignored the question.

"We have three distinct families," Erendira kept reminding me. "There are our two original families—and then there's *our* family. I love that you're still connected to your original family. I love that you love and honor your mom and dad. I love and honor mine. My mom and sisters and their kids are over here all the time. That's great. That's how I want it to be. But then there has to be some kind of separation. That's what they call healthy boundaries. We have to protect the integrity of our family. We have to create an emotional climate where we can breathe freely."

I argued that psychology isn't my strong suit. I'm a practical man. I'm a doer, an activist rather than an analyzer. I pointed out that I have an agenda that will benefit *all* our families.

———

That discussion took place months ago. But now, as I go through the final stages of my Walk Across America, there is no more discussion. I'm on the road and Erendira is home with no interest in talking to me.

Heartbroken and confused, I consult my closest friends.

"It's obviously about more than that one comment," says my buddy Mike Duff.

"That one comment was stupid," I say.

"Especially since you knew that she was out in the car listening to the interview."

"I was just being flip."

"It happens. From time to time, we all shoot from the hip. But this thing has been building."

"I really didn't see it coming."

"That's part of the problem. You're not really thinking about her. You're so preoccupied with getting where you want to go that you don't have time to feel what she's going through."

"No one can accuse me of not putting family first," I argue. "For me family is everything."

"You keep saying that, Nik, and I believe you. But that's both a generalization and a cliché. Sure, it's good to build up your career and save your money and provide for your family. Sure, you can be loyal to your wife—and I know you are— but that doesn't mean that you don't take her for granted."

"I tell her all the time..."

"It isn't what you tell her, it's how you act. If you act like she's simply another member of your team—as opposed to your equal partner—then I can understand her frustration. She's a woman with gifts and talents of her own. Those gifts and talents need to be recognized. She has emotional needs. You need to see that before it's too late."

I go through weeks of sleepless nights, afraid that I have irreparably damaged the one thing more precious to me that any other: the love of my wife.

In my confusion, I seek God's Word. I speak with an

older man with a deep scriptural wisdom who suggests that I look at Matthew 20:26–28:

> *But whoever would be great among you must be your servant, and whoever would be first among you must be your slave, even as the Son of Man came not to be served but to serve, and to give his life as a ransom for many.*

Then he points to Matthew 23:11–12:

> *But he who is greatest among you shall be your servant. And whoever exalts himself will be humbled, and he who humbles himself will be exalted.*

And Philippians 2:3–5:

> *Let nothing be done through selfish ambition or conceit, but in lowliness of mind let each esteem others better than himself. Let each of you look out not only for his own interests, but also for the interests of others. Let this mind be in you which was also in Christ Jesus.*

The Scripture that perhaps speaks loudest of all is 1 Peter 3:8–9:

> *Finally, all of you be of one mind, having compassion for one another; love as brothers, be tenderhearted, be courteous; not returning evil for evil or reviling for reviling, but on the contrary blessing, knowing that you were called to this, that you may inherit a blessing.*

The concept, of course, is humility. Humility keeps coming up. I have no problem humbling myself before God, but how about the world?

After fifteen separate superdramatic skywalks in the past three months, after all the recognition in the press and acclaim from the fans, the world seems to be doing all it can to boost my ego. Or maybe I'm the one who's doing all I can to assert myself.

For a guy who is supposedly an expert on maintaining balance, I feel like I'm losing it. I'm off-kilter. My life has been tilting to one side—my side. How to correct the imbalance? How to negotiate the most challenging walk of all—the walk of life?

Having thousands of people cheering me is a wonderful thing. Applause excites all entertainers—and I'm no different. We seek applause at every turn. But the one person who is not applauding is the one who means the most.

When I return home to Sarasota, Erendira is still sullen.

"I've prayed about all this," I say.

"So have I."

"I love you."

"Our love has never been in doubt," she says.

"And I'm truly sorry about what I said on the radio."

Erendira stays silent.

"I know you feel neglected," I say.

"It isn't a matter of neglect."

"Well, maybe 'neglect' is the wrong word."

"Try *controlled*. I feel controlled."

"And I feel like my ego has been controlling me. Or maybe it's my fear that if I can't control my own family, I won't be able to control what happens out there on the wire."

"Or maybe it's just how you've been raised. You were born into a family ruled by one man."

"And so I tried to become that man."

"You did more than try, Nik. You became that man."

"And I can become a different man."

"How?"

"First by recognizing how my attitude is stifling you. Recognizing that chauvinism is chauvinism. Chauvinism is machismo and sexism and all that other stuff. It doesn't matter if I was born with chauvinism or just developed it. I had it."

"*Had?*"

"Okay, have. But that doesn't mean it's a permanent condition."

"It's an awfully hard one to lose," says my wife. "It's a burden."

"It's a burden I can take to God. Through prayer, through meditating on God's Word, through long hours alone, Erendira, I'm seeing through this thing. I really am. We tell people that we're born-again Christians, and we are. But being born-again isn't a one-time thing. We're continually being reborn with new insights about our struggles and behavior. God is always revealing Himself to us, always opening windows and doors that shed new light. I think I've been living in some dark places. I've been so desperate to make my mark that your emotions weren't a priority. I saw you as someone who loved me and was willing to go along for the ride."

"I do love you, Nikolas. And I am willing to go on this ride, as long as you remember it's our ride, not just yours."

"I've been trying to remember that. I've been working on finding a way to make peace between the demands of my ambition and my desire to walk humbly as a servant of Christ."

"I'm so happy to hear that, sweetheart, but only time will tell whether those are just words."

"Those are words I mean with all my heart."

"Then if you let your heart lead the way, we'll be okay."

"My heart has been longing for you ever since you left me in Ohio."

"My heart is smiling now, Nikolas. My heart is feeling that you're really willing to change."

## 16

# Sizzle

I want to change. I will change. I do change. I realize that there's a difference between determination and pigheadedness. I also realize there's a difference between being a strong and responsible father and being an emotional brute.

Because I'm driven beyond normal reason, I see that my drive at work—my need to supervise my crew and make certain every last detail is perfect—cannot and should not apply to my life at home.

It's easy for me to see this fault in others. I can appreciate the CEO of an international conglomerate who spends his days giving orders and maintaining control of his sprawling concern. He has to run his company like clockwork. When he gets home it's hard for him to turn off his CEO mode. And when he barks orders to his wife and kids like they're his underlings, it's reprehensible. The scenario repulses me.

And though I'm a far cry from a CEO, I can see that I have the same problem flipping the switch from the outside world, which requires a rough-and-ready attitude, and the inside world—the world of my home, my wife, and my precious children—which requires infinite patience, care, and love.

Just like the CEO, I face a battery of challenges every waking day. My life on the line depends on exactitude. There is no room for mistakes, no matter how small. That requires that I scrutinize everyone and everything. As a performer, this is what I learned from my mom. As a rigger, this is what I learned from my dad. In my line of work, being demanding is not only smart, it's essential to your physical survival.

But what about the emotional survival of a family?

Emotions aren't exact; they're messy. Feelings can't be understood in mathematical or scientific terms. It's hard for me to put this into action, but the emotions and feelings of others must always be considered. When I closely study the life of Jesus, I see Him meeting people on their own terms. I see Him listening, understanding, and offering extraordinary compassion. He doesn't treat his team of disciples like a workforce to be ordered about. He treats them as brothers. He is not a harsh taskmaster but rather a loving teacher who has time for everyone. He radiates patience. He embodies love.

This is my goal: to be a loving husband, father, son, and friend. I don't want to be some domestic tyrant who, having been the demanding boss all day at work, can't turn it off at night.

Still, I struggle. Jumping from one role to the other isn't easy. Being demanding, being controlling, being in charge of my world is heady business. It can feel good. It can give me the impression, although false, that I've gotten a handle on the chaotic nature of things. I'm running things—and I like that.

Who doesn't?

Especially when things seem to be going my way.

———

That's what happened to me at the very start of the Walk Across America when I was in Marion, Ohio. I got a call from a TV production company in L.A.

"You're brilliant," said the head of the firm. "You're a superstar. You're everything that America wants to see on TV."

Like most people, I'm a fool for flattery. But this flattery was especially seductive since it came with an offer.

"You're a dreamer, aren't you, Nik?"

"I have dreams, yes."

"And those dreams are about doing bigger and better things."

"That's right."

"I think I can help you make many of those dreams come true."

"How?"

"By finding a way to finance them."

"I'm interested."

"Then let's talk."

We do. I learn that the man wants to package and sell me as a series to Discovery Channel. Each episode will show me developing and then executing a new and daring feat. The feats will grow more daring with each passing week.

How do I feel about having cameras follow me during every stage of my stunts—even the preparation?

I'm fine with that. I'm more eager for the exposure than I am concerned about my privacy.

"What do we have to do to get started?" I ask.

"Make a sizzle reel."

"What's that?"

"A short film. A five-minute pitch that not only sells your sparkling personality but gives a glimpse of the heart-pounding drama that you bring to the small screen. Are you game?"

"I am."

We go to work and film the sales pitch for the series. The sizzle reel sizzles. The Discovery Channel is interested. We have some entry-level meetings followed by midlevel meetings followed by a meeting with the big cheese, the president of the network. He says good. He says go. He gives us enough money to film six episodes.

———

A few weeks later I get a call from Winston Simone.

"How'd you like to go to Paradise?" he asks.

"Paradise sounds good."

"The problem is that Paradise is filled with sharks, sting-rays, barracudas, and piranhas."

"Well, that just makes things more interesting," I say.

Winston is talking about Atlantis Paradise Island in the Bahamas. The resort is interested in having me do the first episode of my Discovery series on their property.

I come up with two stunts. The first is riding a bike

on a 260-foot wire above the ocean. That will be a world record—nearly twice the height of my Prudential bike ride in Newark. Guinness will take note.

The second feat will be the longest tightrope trip of my career. I'll take a long walk between the two iconic Atlantis towers over some of the fiercest man-eating fish on the planet.

I'm revved up and ready to go.

Before Paradise, though, I go back to Sarasota, where I do my first hometown skywalk. In downtown Sarasota, I walk from the roof of One Watergate Condominium to the top of the Ritz-Carlton. At Circus Sarasota I also re-create the seven-person pyramid. But during an extension of that engagement in Fort Myers I roll and crack my ankle while playing tennis. It swells up to where I can't lace up my wire shoes. The doctors say it's fractured and requires a cast. A cast will mean that I'll have to cancel the seven-person pyramid; I have no one to replace me as the anchor. I think of my great-grandfather's reaction after the pyramid fell in Detroit. He left the hospital and returned to the circus the very next day. With Karl in mind, I decide to let the ankle heal on its own. It's painful, but I manage. The show goes on, there are no mishaps, and the ankle heals remarkably quickly.

———

More important, I also need healing in my relationship with Erendira. I not only need to reconfirm her faith in me, I need to express my faith in her—her independence and her special gifts. None of this is possible without God.

My struggle with ego and arrogance is continuing. Sometimes I can catch myself getting control crazy; sometimes I can't. When arrogance pops up, I try to acknowledge it. I can own it, but I can't entirely defeat it. Ego has energy of its own. I'm assertive. I'm aggressive. I'm ambitious. I can't stop striving to outdo myself. That won't change. But what can change is my prayer life. I can pray to increase my awareness of when there's too much me and not enough thee. I can try and strike a balance between desire for improvement and desire for adulation.

I want to be noticed. Without that need I'd never last a day as a daredevil performer. The need for the spotlight is in my DNA. But so is my need for God and God's grace. I need to remember that, with or without spectacular achievement, the loving arms of Jesus are always open to me. Spectacular achievement just happens to be my job. But no matter how grand the spectacle, it pales in comparison to the work of the Creator.

Yes, I have a job to do. Yes, I was born to do that job. And yes, the aim of that job is to thrill people by performing seemingly impossible feats. But, in realizing those feats, if I fail to reflect the glory of God I have accomplished nothing.

My ego-driven vanity is not going to disappear. I can't wish it away and I can't entirely pray it away. But can I accept it without indulging it? Can I say, "Hey, I'm a human being. Human beings, mired in insecurity and assaulted by uncertainty, look for all sorts of validation. There's nothing wrong with it—as long as I don't ego-trip myself to a spiritual death; as long as I realize that my spiritual growth, set against my high-profile career, is always going to be a work in progress; as long I continue to do that spiritual work."

———

"I think your two feats in one day will be mind-blowing," says Michelle Wiltshire, head of Atlantis marketing and a wonderful supporter. "They'll bring out the press and heighten interest in the natural resources we've brought to the resort. How many interviews are you willing to grant?"

"As many as it takes to draw a huge crowd."

The crowd arrives early that morning. The plan is to do the bike ride in the morning and then skywalk in the afternoon.

The bike ride is wonderful. I cherish the sight of the deep-blue Caribbean spread out before me. I like the heat. The warm sun in my face is a delight. Pedaling my way across with a slow and steady ease, I feel the presence of God—in the sky, in the sea, in my heart. When I reach my destination at the end of the ride, I wave to the cheering spectators below and thank God for the endless energy of His universe.

My plan is to now relax for the rest of the afternoon. I do just that, but a half-hour before it's time for my evening walk something happens that rocks my world:

I get a call saying that my dad has passed out. An ambulance has been called. My first thought is that he's had a heart attack. I rush over to see him. He's still unconscious. His face is ashen. He looks weak. I'm afraid for his life. The medics arrive. His vital signs are okay but they don't know what's wrong. They put him on a stretcher and carry him into the ambulance. My dear friend Chris Ripo, a professional fireman, is with me.

Meanwhile, the wind whips up and the weather turns bad.

Do I get into the ambulance with Dad? Do I cancel the event? I only have a minute to decide.

"Without knowing my dad's condition, I'm not sure I can do that walk," I tell Chris.

"I understand."

"And he won't be there to do the final checks on the rigging."

"It's your decision, Nik," says Chris. "I'm with you either way."

I close my eyes, which are filled with tears, and stay quiet for ten seconds.

"No," I say, "I gotta do it. That's what my family does. That's what Dad would want."

"Then do it," says Nik. "I'll ride with him in the ambulance."

Chris and I embrace. I kiss Dad on the forehead and run off to the site of the event.

The walk is between the two iconic Atlantis towers. It's the greatest distance of my skywalking career—some two thousand feet. Before I take my first step, I look out on the horizon. Thunderclouds have moved in. Off in the distance, bolts of lightning electrify the sky.

The fact that I will be walking between these two towers over sharks and barracudas is not the issue. Neither is the weather. I've walked through storms before. I've been trained to walk through storms. It's my father's condition that weighs on my mind. It's the fact that my father is not double- and triple-checking the rigging. It's his absence that I'm feeling.

There's a far larger crowd than there was for the bike ride over the ocean. The spectators have arrived with umbrellas and raincoats. As I climb up the rope, there's a light mist. It's sprinkling. The dark thunderstorms have passed but the air is still unsteady. The winds are strong. When I arrive at the top, I look down for my father's customary thumbs-up sign and suddenly remember what, in the moment, I had forgotten. He isn't there.

God is there. God is here. God is everywhere. God is the blood coursing through my veins. God is the excitement in my heart. God is every blink of my eyes, my every breath, my every step. God is the creator of every person watching me, the creator of the stingrays and the piranhas, the master architect, the master poet and painter, the loving master who has imbued me with gifts, just as He has imbued every living soul with gifts, the Father who has fed my faith and allowed me to take this walk over two thousand feet of wet cable—in spite of the whipping winds and the steady rain, in spite of my anxiety about my dad, in spite of all the elements that might throw me off, I maintain balance.

Two hundred feet into the walk, four hundred feet, a thousand feet—step after step after step—I praise the living God. I'm practically trotting over the cable as I pray for the well-being of my dad. I pray for the well-being of my wife and children, for all those watching me, for all who have come to Paradise Island to relax, to renew their spirit, to seek inspiration. I pray that I might inspire and be inspired by acts of courage and faith.

In a final burst, soaking wet, I complete the walk. Chris Ripo is there with a cell phone in his hand.

"It's your dad," he says.

I take the phone and hear him say, "I'm fine, son. Just fine."

"You sure?"

"It was nothing more than heat exhaustion. Glad you didn't cancel. I wouldn't have liked that."

"I know," I say, so happy and so relieved, "and just thank God that you're okay."

———

The Wheel of Steel reclaims its original name—the Wheel of Death—and I decide to incorporate it in my act in Atlantic City. I don't use that name to be overdramatic, but only to be historically accurate. Ringling Brothers thought it sounded too dire. They cleaned it up for public relations purposes. But I believe that the public relates best to artists who, in an attempt to raise the stakes on entertainment, are willing to stare death in the face. Besides, it's a good title for an episode in my Discovery series.

"Do you feel like you're defying God?" a skeptical reporter asks me before the show that starts with a tightrope walk across the shopping center at the Tropicana.

"Not at all," I say. "Why should I defy a God I love?"

"You're doing things that mortals weren't meant to do."

"According to who?"

"According to the laws of reason."

"I look at my work in the most reasonable light possible. I am blessed to have uncles who are noted engineers, men of reason, who tell me whether my feats are practical and possible. My uncle Mike, for example, is a genius, and operates at the highest level of the engineering profession."

"But if you aren't testing God or defying God, aren't you defying death?"

"I'm affirming life. I'm saying that life is about risk— and moving to the next level is about assuming risk. I'm saying that it's good to break through boundaries. When you see someone do something that has been called impossible, you're inspired to attempt the impossible. Sure, there are voices of doubt and despair. I have them. Everyone does. But those voices, though powerful, are self-defeating. They get you nowhere. They make you retreat. I'm not about to retreat. I'm not about to give up. My mantra is never give up!"

"You must know that not everyone watching you is hoping that you make it," says the reporter. "They've come out to be witness to what could be a catastrophe. Isn't that the lure?"

"I don't believe it is. I believe the lure is—*hey, this guy is showing some determination and that makes me feel like I have to be determined as well.* I can't speak for everyone who comes to my shows, but I feel like the overwhelming majority is cheering me on. They don't want me to fall. They want me to succeed."

"And you really don't think it's a matter of showing them how close you can get to the face of death?"

"I'm not looking at death," I explain. "I'm not thinking of death. It's not challenging a negative. It's asserting a positive. When I'm in the middle of a walk or on the wheel, my heart is in a whole different place. I see it as physical poetry. It's an artistic expression. It's uplifting. When I do these feats, my spirit soars. I'm hoping that what I do lends life—which can be mundane and boring—a certain beauty. Inspired by God, the human spirit can soar. That's the point I'm trying to make."

"What's the point of walking a high wire across a shopping mall?"

"It was a whim," I say. "I came here and saw that the ceilings were painted to look like a sky. I loved that look. It made me think that I'd like to climb up into that sky and give the shoppers something to look up to—something that might make their day even brighter, a memory they could bring home, a story they could tell to their friends and neighbors. I thought it would be fun."

It is fun. In the middle of the walk I drop to my knee—and then turn over on my back. I slowly get up and, rather than walk forward, walk backward. I feel suspended in time, suspended in space. I feel free.

That same day I'm on the roof of the Tropicana, twenty-three stories above the boardwalk, where I climb atop the Wheel of Death. I walk inside the wheel as it rotates a dozen times. I climb out, put on a blindfold, and then climb atop the turning wheel, where I jump rope. That makes me feel like a little boy. And again I feel free.

Guinness is back to report that a new world record has been set: No one has ever performed on the wheel at this height.

It's another one for the books. It's good to be making news, it's good to be back in the good graces of my wife, it's good to have my children with me, as I was with my parents, traveling from city to city. Continuity is good. Tradition is good. Family is good. Family is everything. And family history is still driving me, still haunting those dreams that continue to amaze me. Even more amazing is how my dream life and real life are suddenly intersecting.

What can it all mean?

## 17

# Dreaming Reality

I wake up and can't remember my dream, but I know it was about my great-grandfather. He was taking me somewhere, speaking to me, urging me on. I want to recall the specifics. I want to know what it all means.

"Were you a little boy in the dream or a grown man?" Erendira asks me at breakfast.

"I can't remember. I think both."

"Were you frightened? Happy? Excited?"

"Excited."

"Then it was a good dream."

"I've dreamt about Karl a thousand times, but this was different."

"You're always dreaming about him and Niagara Falls. Were there any waterfalls in the dream?"

"There was water!" I suddenly remember. "Water was definitely part of the dream."

"Then it's probably that same Niagara Falls dream."

"The dream," I say, "that won't go way."

—

*"Have you ever thought about walking across Niagara Falls?"*

The question shocks me. Am I hearing this man correctly or am I putting words in his mouth?

"Would you mind repeating the question?" I ask.

"I said, have you ever considered setting up a tightrope and walking across Niagara Falls?"

I'm in my booth at the International Association of Amusement Parks and Attractions convention. I'm there to attract new bookings. I'm used to entertaining all sorts of inquiries, but this one has me floored.

"I've not only thought of it," I say, "I've dreamt of it."

"Well, dreams come true," he says, "if you want them bad enough."

"I want this one real bad."

"Then let's talk."

We do. He says that he has the political clout to make it happen.

—

"It can't happen," my father says. "You need two countries to agree—the U.S. and Canada."

"The man says he has the right connections," I argue.

"Two countries," my father reminds me, "with two political systems that invite dissent. You have the involvement of the state of New York and the province of Ontario. You have governors and senators and parks commissioners. You have a cast of dozens of politicians, any one of whom can pull the rug from under you."

"I want to believe this will work."

"And I don't want to see your heart broken, son."

"My heart's pretty strong."

"I know that, Nik, but look at this thing objectively. Too many obstacles stand in your way."

"Isn't it all about overcoming obstacles?"

"Yes, as long as you have a fighting chance. Even if by some miracle you resolve the political issues, there's the money. Do you have any idea what it would cost to rig cable over the Falls?"

"I have some notion."

"Take a guess."

"A half million."

"Double that," says Dad. "More than double that."

"Discovery will go for it."

"I doubt it. It's way outside their budget."

Dad's right. "Concentrate on something else," he says. "Something a little less grand. Dreaming is something you do when you're asleep. Reality is what happens when you wake up."

———

But then I have another one of those recurring dreams that involve my great-grandfather. I want to discuss it with my mother.

"Do you think that Karl had any premonition of his death?" I ask my mother.

"No. Why do you ask, Nik?"

"I had a dream where he was on his way to a big event. But then he stopped. He turned to me and said, 'You go ahead. You do it for me.'"

"He witnessed death, of course, when the pyramid fell in Detroit. He had seen many people in the circus die, both relatives and friends. But he never spoke of death and I know he never feared it."

"I'm sure that's true, but it's also true that his own death got more news coverage than probably anything he did in his life. I hate that. I hate for that to be the last image of him. How many times have you heard someone say they watched it on YouTube?"

"I hear that all the time."

"I think we should change that."

"What are you talking about, Nik? How in the world are you going to do that? People are fascinated by tragedy."

"By turning tragedy to triumph. By going to Puerto Rico and recreating the walk."

"The same walk where he fell?"

"The same walk, the same height, the exact same spot. I want to do it."

"And you don't think you'll be tempting fate?"

"I don't believe in that kind of fate. I don't think it's any of our fates to fall. It wasn't his fate. It was the fault of his rigging. You and Dad have told me a hundred times that his rigging was wrong. Well, this time Dad and I will be there to make sure that the rigging is right."

—

There are dissenters. There are those who say there is something perverse or even exploitative about replicating my great-grandfather's walk in Puerto Rico.

"Nik's trying to cash in on a catastrophe," says one relative.

"Nik's opening an old wound," says another.

"Nik's looking to glorify himself by pointing out Karl's mistake."

I understand the opposition. Not everyone has to think the way I do, but, from my perspective, my vision is clear:

I'm going back to rectify history. It's a multigenerational feat of love. I feel Karl's spirit encouraging my every move. He doesn't want to be remembered as someone who has fallen, but someone whose dynasty has redeemed his lifelong passion for creative and daring entertainment.

Yet the negative voices persist.

"Don't let those voices get you down," says Erendira.

"I don't feel down," I say. "I feel the same way Karl must have felt when after the collapse in Detroit he left the hospital and showed up at the circus the very next night."

"Someone said to me the other day, 'Your husband is just doing it for the press.' I said, 'Of course we want press. That's part of our business.'"

"Karl died in the very act of getting press," I say. "He did the walk in Puerto Rico because attendance was down. He needed media attention to sell tickets. Now I want media attention to show the world that the Wallendas never give up."

The Discovery Channel agrees with me. They like the idea and grant final approval. This dream will become real.

The dreams stop just when I think they would have intensified. With so many of my thoughts on my great-grandfather and his final act, I almost expect him to reappear in some sort of sleeping vision. But he doesn't. I'm left alone with my thoughts. I can focus on nothing but this hundred-foot-long walk between the two ten-story towers of the Condado Plaza Hotel in San Juan.

My parents and I go down for an initial visit. We meet with the city officials and the hotel executives. We look over the site. For a walk of this kind, it is relatively routine. But because of its history, the walk will be anything but routine. The press picks up the story and plays it for all it is worth. The city and hotel see it as a boon for business. Tourists will flock to the event. Television will cover it live.

Yet the negative voices persist.

"They're waiting to see history repeat itself," says one detractor. "They're waiting to see Nik fall. That's the story they're hoping for. That's what all the interest is about."

I refuse to believe that. What I believe is that those following the story are harboring the same hope I am: that history will be rewritten and flip the script from negative to positive.

When we arrive in San Juan for the big event, we're in a positive mood. The day before, we place a plaque on the roof of the building from which Karl began his walk. It's a somber ceremony, a beautiful moment. We release a hundred white balloons into the clear blue sky. Before we leave, Mom turns to me.

"There's something in my heart saying that I want to do this walk with you, Nik."

I'm taken aback.

"Are you sure, Mom?"

"I'm absolutely sure. I've been praying about it. I'm feeling that it's something we must do as mother and son. It's something I have to do as his granddaughter. I need the closure."

I'm surprised and pleased at the same time. So is Dad.

"I'd love to do the walk with you, Mom," I say. "I think it's a beautiful idea."

And so we do. On the day of the walk, my dad, the crew, and I spend hours on constructing, checking, and rechecking the rigging.

Mom stands atop one tower. I stand atop the other. We step onto the wire and walk toward each other. Karl is on my mind. Karl is in my heart. I know the same is true of Mom. We meet in the middle, and she pauses to sit on the wire. We exchange smiles. Then I step over my mother and walk toward the other tower. On the spot where Karl fell, I stoop down and kneel. I send his spirit all the gratitude and love at my command as I blow a kiss and say, "*Vati* Karl, this one is for you."

When the walk is completed, I feel a connection that is both comfortable and overwhelming. This work is done, and that feels great, but I'm also feeling the need for a greater work—Niagara Falls.

—

"I don't think Niagara Falls is going to happen," says one political ally.

"Why not?" I ask. "We have the support of Jim Diodati,

the mayor of Niagara Falls. We have the support of Senator George Maziarz, the third-highest-ranking state senator in New York. He's sponsoring the bill."

"He's a Republican and the governor's a Democrat. The senator is sponsoring the bill that will allow you to start your walk from the American side but the governor can veto it."

"And you think he will?"

"I think he might. The internal skirmishes between parties on the state level are endless. These politicians are entangled in the most Machiavellian schemes you can imagine."

"But the argument against it is so weak."

"The argument has been strong enough to keep both countries from allowing it. The argument has gone on for centuries. They say that a publicized walk will encourage copycats—and that could lead to endless tragedies."

"That's ridiculous. This isn't simply jumping off a cliff. This is constructing a mammoth rigging mechanism that involves the most exacting and advanced engineering. Do you think the average copycat has that kind of knowledge or resources?"

"You're preaching to the choir, Nik. The senator has already drafted what he calls a one-time exemption to the state's antistunting law. He's on your side. He's certain it will do wonders for tourism in western New York. He's working for it passionately. The guy's persistent but the one thing he can't control is the governor. Their constituencies are completely different."

"But what do you think the chances are?"

"No telling."

"I don't want to discourage you, Nik. I'd never discourage you, but, man, the way things are lining up it sounds like Niagara is gonna be even tougher than you had imagined," says my pal Mike Duff.

"To be honest, Mike, I never imagine difficulty. I just imagine doing it. I remember someone once saying that imagination isn't anything more than the images you make up in your mind. Well, I've been making up the image of me walking across those Falls my whole life."

—

It's one thing to find a political solution, but it's another to find the finances. To rig the walk I envision—extending across the widest and most dramatic section of the Falls— will require a custom-designed mechanical construction of enormous proportions. The cost will be well over a million dollars. To underwrite the effort will require the sponsorship of network television.

"Do you think the Discovery Channel would underwrite Niagara Falls?" I ask my manager Winston.

"We'll have to see. The first episode of the series airs next week. It all depends on the ratings."

That initial episode—covering the Atlantis Paradise Island resort feats—has been edited without my input. It highlights those moments when I lose my temper and go off on my crew. I do lose my temper, and it is something I regret, but not with the frequency portrayed here. I understand that drama requires conflict. This depiction, however, is designed to show me as some intemperate diva. Maybe I simply don't want to face my true self, but I don't think so. I think this is reality television's way of creating its own reality, one in which disagreement and dissent keep the viewer hooked.

There's nothing I can do about it and, even worse, there's nothing I can do when I learn that the network is dropping the series. The five other episodes that they've shot will remain on the shelf.

"Were the ratings lousy?" I ask David Simone.

"No, the ratings were fine."

"Then why am I being dropped?"

"They're not saying. But somehow you're off the schedule."

That means my tribute walk to Karl in Puerto Rico will not be shown on national television. It also means that my appearance at Silver Dollar City in Branson, Missouri, won't be shown either. For that appearance, which required months of painful training, I devised an elaborate act hanging from a helicopter that flew 250 feet above ground. The stunt played out in stages. A trapeze was attached to the chopper. I grabbed on to the trapeze and supported my body with both arms. Then I let go and used only one arm. Then I released my arms and hung by my legs. And then I hung only by my teeth, setting my sixth world record. My neck ached for weeks afterward.

It was in Branson that I also executed a three-person chair pyramid. A colleague and I rode bikes across the high wire while my mother sat atop a balance bar that we carried on our shoulders. That wasn't difficult. What was tough, however, was to pretend that, in the middle of the ride, we were losing balance and Mom was in danger of falling. The audience loved the thrill of a near-spill, but dramatizing ineptitude proved to be an art in and of itself.

"So none of this is going to be shown?" I ask my manager.

"Nothing. It's all scrapped."

"And Niagara Falls?"

"It's not going to happen with Discovery. We're going to have to find another way."

—

NBC said yes to my Grand Canyon walk and then said no. Discovery Channel said yes to a series, ran one episode, and then said no. What in the world was going to make me believe that Niagara Falls, by far the most difficult of any project I've ever imagined, had even a remote chance?

"I don't want to see your heart broken again," says my mother.

"You know how I feel," says Dad. "It's a pipe dream."

"How do you feel about it, Nik?" my managers ask.

"Where there's a will there's a way," I say.

I'm not thinking of my will. I'm thinking of God's. I don't mean that God is personally intervening in the minds of the politicians and money men who will determine whether this Niagara Falls walk can actually happen. I mean that God is opening my heart; I'm looking to God to assuage my fears so I can pursue this passion with clarity and strength.

I'm reading James 1:6–8, which says, "But let him ask in faith, with no doubting, for he who doubts is like a wave of the sea driven and tossed by the wind. For let not that man suppose that he will receive anything from the Lord; he is a double-minded man, unstable in all his ways."

I pray for single-mindedness. I pray that I might faithfully pursue what I think is reasonable and right. It's reasonable that I walk across Niagara Falls. I've skywalked great distances before. There is wind and rain and uncertain weather, but I've faced such obstacles before. It is right that I attempt this feat, just as my great-grandfather was right in pursuing his own grand schemes. He lived for the realization of spectacular events. I live for the same. He took it as far he could. I must do the same.

Fate has kicked me in the head before. Fate will surely kick me in the head again. Fate is fickle, whimsical, ever-changing. Fate is beyond my control. Looked at from a distance, fate can seem funny. Detached from my ego, fate doesn't have to appear unfair or punishing. Fate is merely the accumulation of circumstances created by others.

I seek to create my own circumstances. I seek to force fate in my direction. I seek to stay so steady in my course— so single-minded, so obsessively positive—that fate will bend my way. And if I am diligent at this task, if I continue to praise God and exhibit His love in all my encounters, no matter how challenging they might be, what could possibly go wrong?

Try everything.

# 18

# The Falls

I read Romans 15:4, which says, "For whatever things were written before were written for our learning, that we through the patience and comfort of the Scriptures might have hope."

I take "before" to mean not only the days of the Old Testament, but the former days of my family—not only my great-grandfather but his great-grandfather, Johannes the acrobat, his grandfather Karl, his father, Englebert—all entertainers, all men striving for accomplishment and recognition, all dedicated to pushing the limits of the possible, all pioneers into the territory of the unknown.

Politics is the territory of the unknown. Network television is the territory of the unknown. Politicians and media moguls are strange animals, motivated, like everyone else, by survival. Their job is to take the public pulse and respond accordingly. They chase the elusive prize of popularity. Sometimes they win the prize, often they don't.

Either way, they are influential and powerful people who exude absolute certainty about the uncertainty of what the people really want.

I believe that there are a substantial number of people who want me to walk across Niagara Falls. I think the walk, done well, would entertain and even thrill them. I think my plan is sound: to rig the cable across the deep two-hundred-foot gorge in the Niagara River, going from Goat Island on the American side to Table Rock on the Canadian side. To my right would be the American Falls and to my left the enormous Horseshoe Falls of Canada. The site would lend itself to the most awesome camera angles imaginable. It's a natural for television coverage.

The politics, beginning with the state of New York, hit a hopeful note. The state Senate approves a bill sanctioning the walk. The state Assembly approves the same bill. In both houses there is very little opposition. Now it's up to Governor Cuomo, who has ten days to either sign or ignore the bill. To ignore it is to kill it.

Negative voices—there are always negative voices—predict that, as a Democrat, he will not sign a Republican-initiated piece of legislation.

With nine days to go, there's no word.

"How long does he usually take to decide whether he'll sign or not?" I ask a politically informed friend.

"Hard to predict."

"He won't wait till the last moment, will he?"

"Probably not. If he likes the bill, he'll probably approve it in the first few days."

Eight days to go, no approval.

Seven days to go, not a word.

Six days to go, still nothing.

"Are you sure that no early approval means that he wants to veto it?" I ask my friend.

"It doesn't look good, Nik. If he wanted to sign, he would have done so by now."

Five days to go before the deadline, then four days, then three—silence.

I keep calling, I keep hoping.

Two days to go.

"Would he possibly wait this long?" I ask.

"I don't see why he would. I think the bill's as good as dead."

One day to go.

"Do you think he's going to sign it, Nik?" asks Erendira.

"I think he is."

On the last day he does.

On to the Canadian side of the political fence.

———

In the summer of 2011, more than a year after my Niagara Falls push began, the board of the National Parks of Canada has made a decision. (In Canada it is the government-appointed NPC, and not a legislative body, that has jurisdiction over the Falls.) The decision is that their anti-stunting restriction will stand. They will not allow the walk.

I immediately ask if I might personally meet with the twelve-member board. The answer is yes, but not until October.

Come October, my father and I travel to Canada. We are

prepared to argue what seems to me a solid case. We will show how the walk will benefit Canada with not only positive publicity but, more significantly, positive economics. The walk will be a boon to the region's tourism.

I'm told that I have five minutes. Because I have arranged my argument in such a comprehensive fashion, it will take me at least ten minutes. I ask—and am granted—a little extra time.

When my dad and I enter the room and are seated in front of the board, one of the members starts by saying that today there will be a special presentation by Nik Wallenda, who will discuss his proposed walk over Niagara Falls. The member reminds the board that a law prohibits such a walk—and, furthermore, said law has already been reviewed and upheld. However, we have no choice but to allow Mr. Wallenda to state his case.

Quite an introduction.

Undeterred, I calmly and rationally go into all the reasons that this walk makes sense. Slowly but surely I build the argument. I'm about halfway through, when a member interrupts.

"You have one minute to wrap it up, Mr. Wallenda."

"But I was granted some extra time."

"One more minute, Mr. Wallenda, and that's it."

That throws me for a loop, but I do my best to conclude. In midsentence, I'm told by that same member to stop talking.

"Your walk is about sensationalism," I'm told. "And the Falls are not about that. The Falls are about the beauty of nature—not some stunt."

That's when Dad, who is a lot less patient than me, can't help but speak up.

"With all due respect," he says, "this isn't a stunt. This is something that our family has trained to do for over two hundred years. This isn't crawling into a barrel and going over the edge of the Falls. This is athleticism. This is artistry. This is a wondrous feat. So please, out of respect for us and our family history, do not call this a stunt."

My father's words move me—but unfortunately no one else. We're excused. Every indication is that, if anything, the board is more opposed to me now than ever. Before we leave, though, we're told that the board will reconsider the matter and issue a press release with their decision within two weeks. That gives me a glimmer of hope.

As we leave the room, the press is waiting. News reporters from both countries shout out questions.

"How did the NPC react to your presentation, Nik?"

"Did you change their mind?"

"Is there a date for the walk?"

"How did the meeting go?"

I consider the questions and then, in all earnestness, answer, "There are issues that remain, but I'm grateful for the opportunity to have met with the board. I'm grateful that they listened to me, and I think that progress will be made. I believe this walk is something that will entertain not only the people of this region, but the world. The walk is about realizing the impossible, and never giving up, which is exactly my attitude. So yes, I see this is as a good day. I have no doubt ultimately the right decision will be made."

Two weeks later, the NPC board issues a press release.

They have reconsidered the matter and have unanimously decided that Nik Wallenda will *not* be allowed to walk across the falls into Canadian territory.

I consider my options. I could refigure the walk and rig the cable to go from one angle of the American Falls to another angle on U.S. soil. But that isn't my vision. That would also exclude the Horseshoe Falls, the single site people associate with Niagara—not to mention the most awesome. It isn't as good, but it's better than nothing.

When I float the idea, though, I'm told that a high official in the New York Parks Department will not approve it. I'm told that the law passed specifically indicated a U.S. to Canada walk, not a U.S. to U.S. walk.

Another roadblock, another chance to give up the crazy scheme, another opportunity to read the tea leaves as saying, "This isn't supposed to happen."

Or another chance to take it to God.

"Lord, if it's Your will to remove this goal from my heart, remove it," I pray. "If this dream and desire are misplaced or merely my willfulness, let the dream and desire die. Set me free."

I turn to Scripture and find myself at Philippians 3:12–14. "Not that I have already obtained, or am already perfected," Paul wrote, "but I press on, that I may lay hold of that for which Christ Jesus has also laid hold of me. Brethren, I do not count myself to have apprehended; but one thing I do, forgetting those things which are behind and reaching forward to those things which are ahead, I press toward the goal for the prize of the upward call of God in Christ Jesus."

I'm struck by the words "press" and "upward call." I've

been pressing on for so long that I can't envision myself stopping. Maybe I'm fooling myself, maybe I'm misreading the spirit, but it does feel like an "upward call." I don't have the sensation that God is draining me of the dream and desire. The dream and desire are stronger than ever.

I'm pressing on. I'm finding a way to fund an even more comprehensive report on the impact of this walk. I'm employing an independent research firm that, in a few months, will prove that the event will provide the city of Niagara Falls with $120 million in "legacy effects" over the next five years. I'm showing that, with the high probability of network sponsorship, an enormous worldwide audience will view the walk and fall in love with the beauty of the Falls. I'm guaranteeing that I will provide all the essential safety measures to completely protect the environment. I'm showing that the copycat arguments against the walk are bogus. In all my previous feats, no one has ever come along and tried to duplicate what I've done. There's no reason to believe this will happen now. No amateur can even begin to deal with the mechanics of what it takes to rig a line across the Falls.

I've heard arguments that spectators, wanting a closer look, will be pushed over the edge. Ridiculous. Especially since, as I indicate in this report, we will be putting up two layers of fences, one ten feet away from the other, for the very purpose of keeping people from the edge.

All these arguments have been rejected, yet two influential people have been listening to me. The mayor of Niagara Falls and the local member of Parliament like what I have to say. It turns out that the member of Parliament is also the assistant to the Canadian minister of tourism. That's how my dad, our chief engineer, and I are able to get a meeting with the minister in Toronto.

"I'm not against your project," he tells us, "but I can't overturn the decision of the NPC board. What I can do, though, is ask them to meet with you again. I understand that the last time you tried to make your case you were cut short. I can assure you that this time you will have the benefit of a full hearing."

Armed with fresh enthusiasm and new hope, we return to Niagara Falls. Amazingly, the member who opposed us most vehemently is no longer on the board. The atmosphere is entirely different. The dark cloud of skepticism that greeted us before has been lifted. We're allowed to give our long and probing analysis of why this walk, on every level possible, is a good thing. When questioned closely, we see that our answers are greeted with appreciation, not scorn.

The NPC reverses itself. The walk is approved.

I can't explain why the negative member is gone. I can't explain why what was once totally negative is now totally positive. All I can do is praise God for the energy to go forward—and for the light He continues to shine before my eyes.

"By your patience possess your souls"—Luke 21:19.

But the thing about patience is this: Just when you think you've been patient enough, more patience is required.

I have to learn that lesson over and over again.

———

Great news: A *Good Morning America* producer, Morgan Zalkin, read about my passion to walk over Niagara Falls on

Twitter. She went to her boss and set the wheels in motion at ABC. Now the network has agreed to purchase broadcast rights and underwrite the walk. Thank you, Twitter! Thank you, Morgan! Now it's certain. The walk will take place June 15, 2012.

A few months earlier, someone from *Ripley's Believe It or Not!* contacts my managers. They're opening a museum in Baltimore and want me to do a skywalk over that city's harbor. Sounds great. Plans fall into place. The walk will take place three weeks before Niagara Falls.

*Ripley's* proposes that I walk between two four-story buildings. I appreciate the invitation but it sounds almost too simple. I want to find a way to spice things up.

I suddenly have an idea. What if I start out from the roof of one of the buildings and walk a cable to the top of a crane attached to a moving barge set out in the middle of the harbor?

They love it. We're on.

My crew, led by my father, travels to Baltimore to set up the mechanics. I'm in my hotel room the day before the event when my computer shows a Google alert. It's a story concerning the name Wallenda. I click on the link and find myself reading a story that says years before my birth Karl had done a skywalk over the Baltimore harbor!

His walk was configured differently than mine, but the connection is nothing less than cosmic. I'm literally living my dream.

The walk goes well. The turnout is huge. Media everywhere. I'm nearly at the end of the cable where Chris Ripo is standing to greet me.

"Want to see thirty thousand people scream?" I ask Chris.

Before he answers, I do a fake slip. The crowd sends up an enormous scream. I regain my composure and complete the walk. Thunderous applause. Afterward I don't think that much about it. I see myself as a showman and know that an almost-slip adds drama.

The next day, though, the stuff hits the fan.

I get a call from an ABC exec.

"What happened yesterday, Nik? What was that?"

"You mean the slip?"

"Yes, it frightened us to death."

"That was the point. I did it on purpose."

"You're acting was too good."

"What do you mean?"

"You've given the higher-ups over here the impression that it was real. When you walk across the Falls, they want you to wear a safety harness tethered to your clothing."

"I won't."

"You must."

"It's ridiculous. I've never been tethered before. It goes against my method. It cramps my style. And it creates an unnecessary burden."

"Burden? How can a safety device be a burden?"

"Because it's a distraction. For the same reason my great-grandfather never used a safety net. He knew that it doesn't add safety but instead creates a false sense of safety. His brother Willy died by hitting his head on the pole of a safety net."

"We can't possibly run the risk of having you fall in front

of a worldwide audience that we expect to number close to 500 million."

"I've run that risk my entire life. That risk is the essential fact that lends our feats such drama. We risk everything."

"We can't take a chance on broadcasting what could be a fatality."

"Look at the statistics," I say. "Look at history. Compared to deaths in NASCAR, the number of fatalities among aerial artists is minuscule. You don't hesitate to broadcast NASCAR, knowing full well that the possibility of tragedy is hardly remote. Besides, the typical NASCAR racer began driving in his teens. I began walking the wire at two. I have an enormous amount of training and experience. If you look at a mathematically sophisticated table of probabilities, you'll see that the chance of my dying on the job is extremely remote. You can't say the same about a race car driver."

"The viewers relate to the risks assumed by a driver," says the exec. "Every day when they get behind the wheel they run a similar risk. But they don't relate to your risk. They find it especially frightening."

"I realize that," I acknowledge. "And that's another reason why I don't want to kill the thrill of the feat. I don't want to sanitize it."

"Sorry, Nik, but the call is ours—not yours. We're paying for the walk. It'll happen with a safety tether or it won't happen at all."

Because I want it to happen, I cave. I make my objections known to the public because I certainly don't want it assumed that the tether is my idea. Some people, knowing my stubborn streak, predict that, once on the wire, I'll disconnect the hookup and go out there the way I always do—untethered. To be honest, I do consider that for a moment or two. But ABC is taking no chances and is making me sign a contract that enforces the tethering terms. Beyond this, if I'm to respect the integrity of God and call myself a man of honor, I must adhere to the restriction, no matter how repugnant it might be.

I'm also practicing like crazy. At the beginning of June, two weeks before the walk, my dad sets up a long cable over the parking lot at the Seneca Niagara Casino and Hotel where, day after day, I walk under conditions that simulate what I may face on the Falls. Fire trucks are brought in. Water hoses and giant fans are aimed directly at me as I make my way over the cable, back and forth, back and forth.

Because the walk will take place at night, the most advantageous time to attract an international audience, the lighting will add to both the drama and the difficulty of the feat.

Making it even more difficult is this fact: For the first time since I've been doing skywalks, my dad and uncles have not been able to use the most secure agents—guy-wire stabilizers—in the construction. That's because we need to use a much wider cable to deal with the required tension. This will mean that the cable will sway a great deal, adding to the challenge. Setting that cable across the Falls—eighteen hundred feet—is also no easy job. A helicopter is required as well as a giant winch. To prevent twisting, heavy pendulums are attached to the cable every 150 feet. Were it not for the engineering acumen of my brilliant uncles, none of this would be possible.

And yet, even with this incredible achievement, there is

now news that, only a week before the event, all is in vain. Production costs have exceeded the original estimate of $1 million. The overrun is due to the need for two custom cables, one for the actual event and another for practice. The extra money is not there. I'm out of funds.

*The walk is off.*

Through donations from local Niagara Falls businesses, I hustle up the extra money.

*The walk is on.*

But then I learn that another huge chunk of money is needed for a second helicopter firm. The first, hired to set up the cable, did not have the proper licenses to fly through the Falls. A second chopper is required—and that will cost a fortune. I don't have the money.

*The walk is off.*

I post a website asking for donations. In acts of unexpected and deeply appreciated generosity, the public comes through.

*The walk is on.*

The New York Park Commission is claiming that we have not paid the nearly quarter of a million dollars that the state is charging us to use its land. My managers point out that the state did not give them the proper forms in time and that payment is, in fact, forthcoming. The state remains unmoved.

*The walk is off.*

My managers personally make the payments themselves.

*The walk is on.*

The state says the payments did not cover the full amount.

*The walk is off.*

My managers feel certain that ABC will make the extra payments.

*The walk is on.*

ABC refuses.

*The walk is off.*

At the insistence of my managers, ABC changes its mind and wires the money to cover the fees.

*The walk is on.*

My practice continues. My prayer intensifies:

"Dear Lord, keep me focused on Your goodness, Your mercy, Your everlasting love. Keep me from getting too high or too low, too discouraged or too hyper. Keep me from getting sick and tired of the hassles. Keep me in gratitude for the wonders You have set before me. Keep me anchored in Your will. Keep me balanced in Your sense of what is necessary and righteous. Let me deal with the world on the world's terms but let me turn my heart over to You. Be with me, stay with me, comfort me in this great moment of discomfort."

The discomfort was about the continuing struggle, the endless roadblocks that had been thrown up—the people who had opposed me, the backstabbing, the last-minute attempts to undercut what has become my obsession. The on-again off-again tug of war has been tearing at my heart for months. Were it not for God, I would have gone completely crazy.

"Dear Lord, it's all about getting closer to You. Allow that closeness. Allow me to close off the noise of dissent and negativity. Allow me to feel Your goodness and Your grace.

Allow me to relax in the bosom of Your love. Allow my deeds, no matter how big or small, to express Your glory."

—

In the midst of the madness, only a few days before the walk, I look in the paper and see that Bello is performing in the area. This gives me a feeling of both sadness and joy— sadness because we haven't seen each other for years, and joy because I consider him a dear brother.

After the *Today* show triumph and the success of my solo career, Bello and I went our separate ways. There has been unspoken tension between us. Now I see this as a great time for us to reunite. I send him a text. "It's great that we're both in the area," I write. "Let's get together."

Will my overture work? I'm not sure, but I keep hoping. And then—praise God!—I'm in the middle of my practice walk over the casino parking lot before a big crowd and a TV crew from *60 Minutes Australia* when I look up and see that sky-high red crew cut. It's Bello! I immediately call him over.

"Get up here with me," I say.

He does. He gets on the wire, where I put my arm around him and say, "This is the great Bello, one of my closest friends and the world's foremost daredevil clown."

Everyone cheers. I cheer for Bello, he cheers for me.

There's a postpractice press conference that I insist Bello attend. He agrees. At the conference he stands by my side as I sing his praises.

"Bello's a genius," I say. "This guy is not only one of my teachers, but one of my main inspirations. There's nobody like him. When it comes to innovative, daring feats of courage and beauty, he's the master."

In turn, Bello says a bunch of nice things about me. That night I go to his show. It's a beautiful thing. It's a God thing. Before my big walk, it's a reconciliation that warms my heart. The next day the local paper runs a picture of us walking the wire together, brothers in Christ.

—

On the big day, I awake early, remembering last night's dream. I'm not surprised that my great-grandfather Karl appeared. I'd be surprised if he hadn't. The details aren't clear, but in this dream he was walking with me. He was encouraging and comforting me. He was letting me know that all was well. He was with me last night as I slept and he's with me now as I prepare.

Prayers are in my head. Prayers are in my heart. Erendira and the kids are with me, my mother, my father, my friends.

I spend the day relaxed, focused on the beauty of God, the beauty of breathing, the beauty of offering gratitude to all those who have helped me get ready for this moment.

"Thank you, Jesus, for motivating me, for preparing me, for protecting me, for keeping me steady, for keeping me grounded, for keeping me aloft, for keeping me sane, for keeping me loved."

I eat lightly; I pray continually, silently and out loud; I tend to last-minute details, consulting my dad and the engineers.

I feel the excitement coursing through me. I acknowledge the thrill of anticipation, but I try to stay in the moment.

I'm given a choice: Do I want to be interviewed live by the ABC broadcasters during the walk?

Why not? I'll be wearing a mic, so I don't see that as a problem.

I'm given another choice: During the walk do I want to speak live to my father, who will be watching me through a studio monitor?

Why not? It's always reassuring talking to Dad.

After hearing my positive responses to both questions, another network operative asks whether I'm sure I want to deal with those distractions. It might make for good TV, but will I be endangering myself?

"If it were endangering," I say, "I wouldn't do it. I can talk and walk at the same time."

The network man laughs and wishes me well.

Throughout the day, I keep looking out my hotel window, expecting to see crowds. But the crowds don't come. Only a few tourists are walking around. I've promised the network that tens of thousands of people would appear. Could I have been so wrong? Could it be that there's virtually no interest in this event? Is it possible that after all this incredible work, no one really cares?

At noon, at 2:00 p.m., at 4:00 p.m., even at 6:00 p.m. there is no crowd to speak of.

"This is horrible," I tell Erendira. "No one's coming."

"Patience," says my wife. "It's still early."

I want to believe her, but despair is setting in. I begin to doubt—not my ability to make this walk but my ability to draw the kind of record-breaking crowd that will make it so special.

Then comes the miracle to prove me wrong. At 7:00 p.m., as if on cue, people begin swarming over the grounds. It happens all at once. Thousands upon thousands of people. So many people that I can't see a blade of grass. People—old people, young people, people of every age and color—are everywhere. There are more than twenty thousand people on the American side, my point of departure, and more than one hundred thousand on the Canadian side, my point of arrival.

I'm beyond excited as I consider the task at hand.

Eighteeen hundred feet across.

The widest section of the Falls.

Millions watching worldwide.

Helicopters above, boats below, dozens of cameras positioned to capture the walk from dozens of angles.

Years in preparation. Generations in preparation. Dreams from my childhood. Gifts from my ancestors. Spirits swirling around me. Gusts of wind. An incredible battery of lights. The illumination of a walk. The illumination from God.

All attention on me.

My need, my passion, my joy to put all attention on Him.

I put on the shoes made by my mother, custom-sewn moccasin-ballet slippers designed to give me traction on the wet cable.

I walk to the starting point. I wear a small mic and an earpiece. In my pocket is my United States passport to present to the officials when I reach Canada. Before I step out on the cable, I consider taking off this ridiculous tether. I resist doing so. I let it go. I look out on the Falls—magnificent, eternal, dreamlike. A mighty force of nature. A mighty creation of God.

I take my first step. I enter the zone.

The zone is the place in which God and His glory are manifest everywhere. In the zone you move by instinct, by gentle feeling—nothing is forced, the rhythm determined by the motion that you neither create nor fight. The zone has you moving in an automatic, programmed way. Because you're prepared, the program is to some degree of your own making. But it is so much greater than that. The program has to do with surrendering to the moment. In the moment there is nothing but you and your infinitely small place in the cosmos.

Looking out at this incredible site—the river, the Falls, the lights, the crowds, the boats below and the choppers above—all I could do was praise God. All I could do was tell God Almighty how grateful I was for the gift of my life. I love you, Jesus. You are my Lord. You are my Father. You are my morning star, my beginning and my end, my everything, the shining light of love that has led me ever since I was a little boy old enough to understand that You are the creator of all that is good and right, all that is beautiful and blessed. Blessed be this walk. Blessed be this night. Blessed be this moment in which the magnificence of Your creation is evident to all the world.

The majesty of the view is beyond anything I have ever seen. It is beyond anything I have ever imagined. I see it as God's greatest painting, a landscape of awe-inspiring grandeur. I am aware that never before has a human been in this particular place to drink in this particular view. I am overwhelmed with gratitude.

I pray and praise continually, interrupted from time to time by a few questions from the ABC commentators in the broadcast booth. I assure them that all is well. I'm on course. This is what I do. And yes, there is some heavy wind, and yes, when I get above the Falls themselves, there is a great deal of mist, and yes, this is a little trickier than what I had imagined, but no, nothing I can't handle. Wind and mist and rain are part of the deal. Finding traction on a slick, wet cable is part of the challenge. I don't mind the questions. Yes, I'm happy to speak with my dad. Yes, Dad, all is well. No problems. Let me go on.

Let me keep walking through this vast living dream that has consumed me for most of my life, that is consuming me now, that has me calling out the name of my Savior again and again. This walk is a celebration, an acknowledgment that the indomitable spirit of Karl Wallenda is alive and that you, Father God, are the living Word directing my path. You, Father God, are worthy of all praise, all devotion, all energy. I want to live through You and pray that You live through me. Walk with me, stay with me, Father God, be my comfort and my steady friend, my rock and my redeemer.

The cable bends. The cable sways. The cable curves up and the cable curves down. The wind blows and the mist covers my eyes. Sheets of rain wash over me. But through it all, I'm smiling, my heart is laughing, my heart is singing, my heart is light with the certain knowledge that I serve a righteous God. My heart has never been happier—happy to answer more questions from the commentators, happy to check in again with Dad, happy to keep praying and expressing my boundless love for the Lord.

Some twenty-five minutes after I began, I approach my final destination. I go down on one knee and blow a kiss to the crowd before trotting the last few feet. Erendira, Yanni, Amadaos, and Evita are there to greet me. So is an army of reporters and photographers from all over the world. So is the Canadian official who asks to see my passport. Not having prepared a speech, I simply speak from my heart: My hope is that this walk inspires people throughout the world to achieve their goals and realize their dreams.

The rest is a blur—a good blur, but a blur nonetheless. I remember calling my grandmother, Karl's daughter, back in Sarasota, who said she was too nervous to watch.

"I'm fine," I tell her. "I love you."

I tell my mom and dad, who are by my side, the same.

I tell the TV commentators that yes, the mist was thick, and yes, it was hard to see at times. Yes, the winds got wild, but no, I wasn't frightened and, no, it wasn't anything I hadn't anticipated, and yes, it feels great to be the first person to ever walk over the Falls on a high wire, and yes, this is the highlight of my professional life, yes, this is a dream come true—*the* dream come true.

The next morning I will learn that the international audience—predicted at 500 million—was double that number. The two-hour special garnered an estimated one billion. In the United States alone the Nielsen ratings went through the roof. Viewership records were broken left and right.

And yet, for all the commotion, back in the hotel suite that I shared with Erendira and our children, the one thought that gives me peace and lets me come down from the high of an achievement I had sought for so many years is found in the Word of God.

I pick up the Bible and in 2 Timothy 4:7 I read these words:

"I have fought the good fight, I have finished the race, I have kept the faith."

# 19

# Keeping the Faith

Keeping the faith is all that keeps me balanced. If I didn't believe, I'd fall in any number of ways. By believing, my spirit stays afloat.

The day after the walk over Niagara Falls I keep the faith by returning to Goat Island on the U.S. side to help pick up garbage. I'm careful not to alert any of the publicists surrounding the event that I'm doing this because my purpose is not self-aggrandizement. My purpose is simply to help clean up after myself. The huge crowd left a great deal of trash behind, and I feel compelled to pitch in. Besides, after the inordinate amount of attention I sought and received, I need to keep myself grounded. Three hours of cleaning up debris is good for my soul. Humility does not come naturally to me. So if I have to force myself into situations that are humbling, so be it. Just as I dug the hole that held my anchor on the Canadian side, I make it a point to refill the hole. I know that I need to get down on my hands and knees like everyone else.

"That's just vain humility," a detractor tells me. "You do it because it makes you look good."

"I do it," I say, "because it's a way to keep from tripping. As a follower of Jesus, I see Him washing the feet of others. I do it because if I don't serve others I'll be serving nothing but my ego. I do it for the same reason that I don't travel with an entourage—just my family and a few trusted friends. And for the same reason I fly coach."

"I thought you fly coach because you're too thrifty to pay for first class."

I laugh and say, "Well, that's part of it, too."

Other detractors say that the prayers I spoke during my walk, audible to viewers throughout the world, were a calculated move to appear holier-than-thou. The problem with that argument was that I had no idea that my prayers were being broadcast. I'd been told my mic would be open only when I was responding to questions asked by the ABC broadcasters and my dad. I only learned that they had kept my mic open when the walk was over. I wasn't at all displeased; I had no shame about addressing Christ while on the wire; I had been doing it for years. But it certainly wasn't planned. It wasn't self-conscious.

Now I'm glad that the mic was hot. I'm glad the world heard how, in the midst of my most precarious walk, I turned to Jesus to balance my spirit. I'm glad because of the hundreds of letters and emails I received from people moved by my prayers. I'm glad because the author helping me write this book says he never would have sought this collaboration had he not heard me praying over Niagara Falls. I'm glad because the words came from my heart and expressed the true love and gratitude I feel for my Lord and Savior.

———

Keeping the faith means keeping myself consciously connected to God, even as I consciously understand the precarious position of someone like me who is constantly seeking the spotlight. My ambition has not waned and I'm not sure it ever will. While writing this book I've been preparing to be the first person to walk across the Grand Canyon. Unlike Niagara Falls, there has been no drama concerning permissions and permits. Several networks vied for the rights to broadcast the event. I was delighted when the Discovery Channel emerged the winner, and even more delighted when there was no demand that I be tethered. By the time you're reading this, my hope is that the Grand Canyon walk will be realized and celebrated as an even more spectacular success than Niagara Falls.

I'm a proud product of the circus, proud of my family's circus history and proud to have contributed to the luster of that institution. I'm also proud of my efforts to repackage aerial entertainment in dramatic settings. I've tried to make it modern, inventive, and more exciting. I've tried to take feats that, in the past, might have seemed nerdy and make them cool. Whether I'm walking on a wire or doing handstands inside a Wheel of Steel, I employ old theatrics with new angles and innovative approaches. I do crazy things to get attention and to entertain.

As an American committed to free enterprise, I embrace the ethos of the small businessman. I strive to build my brand. I believe in investing in my future. I believe in saving more than I spend. I work to insure the financial welfare of my family. I'm motivated to increase my ability to earn. I cherish that motivation. I want to do more, make more, entertain more, reach more people.

And yet these are worldly matters. These are, for the most part, material goals that are good and sound. They require strong initiative on my part and a belief in my ability to get better in every aspect of my life. I know that I run the risk that faces every prominent showman. I know that because I've fallen on my face, not as a performer but as a husband and a human being. Many are the times when I've been overly impressed with my own gifts. Over and again, I've had to be right. I've had to have the last word. I've been intolerant when others haven't done what I've wanted them to do. I've been impatient when others haven't moved at the speed that I want them to move. In short, I haven't always been the man that I want to be.

So I go on, seeking a balance between accepting my limitations and seeking improvement in my character. I'm leery of seeking perfection, because, in my mind, to believe in personal perfection is just another expression of egotism. Only God is perfect. And yet we strive, even as we bask in the glow of His unconditional grace, to live in that space that bridges individual achievement and divine acceptance.

To live in that space is to dwell with God, now and forevermore.

# ACKNOWLEDGMENTS

I have great appreciation for so many people who have been influential in my life.

First, I want to express my love to my beautiful and supportive wife, Erendira. You have taught me the true meaning of love, as you have stood by my side through thick and thin, for better or worse. I would not be who I am today if it was not for you and your unending love.

To my son Yanni, who made me a Daddy for the first time, you were an incredible baby boy and have since turned into an even more incredible young man. Amadaos, thanks for being a "Daddy's boy" and keeping me young playing sports in the back yard. To my beautiful daughter Evita, thank you for your sweet heart. You will always be Daddy's baby girl! All three of you are deeply blessed with the favor of God and have an incredibly bright future! Go change the world!

I could not have achieved these heights in career or life without my parents, Delilah and Terry, and my sister Lijana. Mom, thank you for teaching me to walk a wire at a young age; and Dad, thank you for teaching me the proper and safe way to rig a wire and so much more about life. Most important, I thank you both for raising me up in a loving household and showing me, by example, how to serve Jesus Christ my Lord and Savior. Lijana, thank you for being a part of many performances, being supportive of all that I do, and for being my wife's best friend (particularly when I've made a mistake).

Chris Ripo, thanks for being one of the most influential people in my life during my late teenage years, and continuing as adults. You have taught me how to work hard, run a business, and kept me humble. Joseph Mascitto, you are the best friend a man could ask for. Thanks for taking my calls in times of stress, even if they were in the middle of the night. Mike Duff, thanks for being a great friend and, well, for being Mike Duff. After all these years, I think that says it all. Andy Collins, thanks for ignoring the playbook on the football field, and "just throwing me the ball"! To Tim Carlson, you have been my consultant for my rigging supply needs and so much more. Tom Rhein, you have been there to provide words of encouragement since my first performance on the wire to Niagara Falls, and I have the amazing photos to prove it! Bello Nock, thanks for showing me how to not only make a living doing what we do, but to take it to the next level! David Blaine, thanks for your friendship and encouragement through the years! To my Uncle Tom Troffer, thanks for being an example to me of what a real-life superhero is. You taught me everything I know! Uncle Mike, as you are now known to all my crew and the world, thanks for all of your assistance in making sure that every stunt I do is engineered safely and properly.

Shelley Ross, you saw the potential I had to be on TV from the moment we met and introduced me to my amazing managers, David and Winston Simone. David, thank you for your overwhelming support; and, Winston, for believing in me from the very start. The three of you have played a huge role in making my dreams come true!

John Carson, you hired me when I was fifteen and you have always demonstrated that hard work equals reward. Pastor Neville Gritt, thank you for teaching me how to live a righteous life and, to this day, attending my performances whenever possible. Pastor Steven Schlabach, you have continually encouraged me and relentlessly taught and reinforced the word of Grace.

Jim Bell, thanks for giving me my first shot at a live nationally televised stunt as I broke my first individual world record. Matt Lauer, your coverage of my bicycle world record and the words you spoke to me on that couch in the studio will never be forgotten! Jon Rosen, for believing in me since the first day we met in your office.

Morgan Zalkin, thanks for the "tweet" that would eventually lead to the ABC TV special. James Goldston and Ben Sherwood, you guys took a chance on me, and I am forever grateful you took the risk of covering history on live TV. Roger Trevino, your assistance made it possible for me to connect with decision makers in Niagara Falls, New York. To all of the officials and authorities in New York who were brave enough to support me against long odds, Assembly-man John Ceretto, Assemblyman Dennis Gabryszak, Sena-tor Mark Grisanti, and my close friend Senator George Maziarz; to the officials in Canada who bravely trusted from the initial idea, Minister Michael Chan, and my dear friends MPP Kim Craitor, and Mayor Jim Diodati and to NPC Chair Janice Thomson for eventually coming on board and fully supporting me; to Henry Wojtaszek for his legal assistance and, more important, friendship; to John Bar-tolomei for his incredible negotiating skills; to Joel Wein-stein for always having my back; and to all of my Indiegogo supporters, Rick Winter, and David Diamond, for stepping in at the last moment and helping me raise enough money to cover the majority of the expenses for Niagara, you made a life-long dream become a reality. To Phil Sarna for mak-ing sure that everything adds up when we are all said and done! Michael Sourenson and Edward Sabin, thanks for taking hold of the dream for the next endeavor. I am excited to have your support in even greater career steps, this time across the Grand Canyon. The Navaho Nation for granting me permission to fulfill my next dream on your beautiful land!

To my great-grandfather Karl Wallenda, you paved the way to my future and exemplified the "Never Give Up" spirit! It is your legacy I strive to carry on.

Finally, to the hundreds of others who have inspired, believed, trusted, and encouraged me to pursue my dreams and Never Give Up, and to every fan and audience mem-ber who has viewed my performances live or on worldwide media, your cheers drive me to new heights!

Special thanks to the following friends who helped make my Niagara Falls Walk the success that it was.

Matthew Holla
Christine Boyd
Gary Smith
Keith Nelson
Walter Latacki
Lori Franze
Donna Metzger
Fran Krajcovic
Daniel Staples
Michael Leung
Jutta Nelson
Helen Kolodey
Fabrizio Di
    Franco
Terry Shaffer
Agata Purcell
Angie Fournier
Marc Miller
Martha Jacobs
Robert Marchese
Philippe
    Tremblay
Daniel DiPasquale
Marvin Mimms
Dawn Kline
Harry Sharma
Carol Robinson

Eric Hitchcock
Denise Almanza
Bradley Thomas
James Ostlund
Steve Barnes
Don Barnes
Michael
    McDougall
Dolores Koenig
Deborah
    Kuczkowski
Joshua Prezioso
Richard Ramey
Jennifer Mason
Joanna St Jacques
Richard Massey
Shigeko Ishikawa
Albert Rodland
Vera Harrison
Joy Lynch
Joseph Sweigart
Shawn Weber
Diana Fabiano
David Kessler
Patricia Rardin
Elizabeth Dexter
Gary Diehl

Leonard Belsher
Scott Allen
Donald
    Veronneau
James Dahlquist
Shelley Bierfeldt
Manuela Kesseler
Haihong Zeng
Paul Resell
Deborah Gordon
David Dessauer
Kelley Mathews
Seton Katz
Vernon Schneider
Maxine House
Mary Bradley
Sarah Moore
Thomas Banas
Arthur Marshall
Howard Fuchs
Ronald Weisman
Paula Finkelstein
Lori Ryerson
Frank Balcerzak
Rod Kennedy
Vick Hilger
David Sypeck

Marjorie Pannell

Nicole Melander

David Scollnik

Daniel Mack

James Robins

Deborah Miller

John Batchelder

Jeff Liffmann

Fred Gallagher

Peggy Nelson

Geoffrey Bell

Lina Czajkowski

Aidan Cosgrave

Matthew Katz

Suzan Payne

AJ Lopata

Iren Pober

Rita Yousett

Tamara Tkaczuk

Stephanie Sugar

Steve Schreiber

Tom Rhein

Rober Trevino

David Morse

Diane Harter

Joseph Mascitto

Noriko Onoe

David Ritz thanks Nik Wallenda, my brother in Christ, Erendira Wallenda, Delilah Wallenda, Terry Troffer, Jana Burson, David Vigliano, Anthony Mattero, Winston Simone, David Simone, my wife, Roberta, my daughters, Alison and Jessica, my sisters, Esther and Elizabeth. Much love to Jim, Henry, Charlotte, Alden, James, Isaac. Much gratitude to Alan Eisenstock and Harry Weinger, my brothers in Moses, and the Tuesday brothers—Skip, David, Dejon, Juan, Herb, Dennis, Ian, John, Kevin, and Dave.